Parables from the Outskirts of Polite Society

by

J.R. SUMMERS

I recognize the value. I can make the adjustment. Yet I feel like I live on the outskirts of polite society, close enough to get to it but not necessarily feeling a need to be there.

Contact Jerome at: jeromersummers@gmail.com

ISBN:10:1523202963

DEDICATION

I dedicate this book to my grandfather, Samuel White II, and to my mother, Edna White Summers.

My grandfather didn't talk to me. Those were the days when children were to be seen and not heard. But he would let me be with him, follow him around, sit on the floor next to his chair when he had meetings, and listen when he spoke. He demonstrated what it is to be a family man, a praying man, a working man, and a humble leader in our community. Even now I ask myself: *"Am I doing something my grandfather, my elders, and my ancestors would be proud to see me do?"*

My mother was earthy, formidable, and solid as a rock. She was a tireless worker for our community with a strong sense of right and wrong, and justice. She genuinely cared about children and people who could not defend themselves. She would say, *"It is the service you give to others that makes your life more valuable. Where is the greatest need?"* She could smell a lie, or what she called *nonsense* from a mile away. She saw more in us than we did in ourselves. She was pleased but never surprised when any of us excelled at something. She expected that. She always believed in me even when I didn't have it coming. She never put me down, not once, not ever.

I still hear both of them in my head, usually when I should step up, go the extra mile, or do something that should be done that I don't want to do. I thank God for their example and for the time they spent with me.

TABLE OF CONTENTS

Acknowledgements

I would like to thank my readers who I hope will find value and usefulness in their own lives through the stories, lessons, and parables.

There are many people whose prayers, words, and encouragement have been instrumental in the concept and completion of this book. Here are a few of them: My mother, Edna W. Summers - I know I am alive today because of her prayers for me; Deidre Causey and Elizabeth Summers, other family members; Mark Adams for his unwavering support; Nathaniel Richardson, Cathy Tabor, Christine McDougal of Australia, Brett Mudgeway and Erina Tepou of New Zealand for their encouragement; authors Michael P. Fuller, who inspired me to write in the beginning, and Mae Catherine Godhigh, who told me I am an anointed writer; Thomas Sexton who made my laptop work; T'wanna Walker who helped me sequence the stories and gave me a female perspective; Pat Markham who helped with most of the editing and gave far more than I expected or even knew I needed; Michael E. Summers and Michael Hudson who helped with formatting, cover ideas, and gave their endless patience; audio engineers, David Mitchell and D'Angelo Fletcher, for their discerning ears, insights, and fine distinctions; David Jenkins photography of Chicago who met me at 5:00 a.m. to catch the rising sun and then took me to breakfast. There is also deep gratitude to Robert Kiyosaki and his lovely wife whose teachings and classes set my life on a higher path. I hear his words and lessons all through this book. Thank you R.K.

Ultimately I give God the glory where it belongs.

With high regard and genuine affection,

J.R. Summers

Forward

At eight years old my mother told me I think in stories so this book has been simmering for a long time. It's uplifting. It can make you laugh, make you cry, and most importantly it can empower you to make better decisions. Use it as a reference book, a call to action, or just an entertaining read with a kick. A friend told me this is her guide to being a grownup.

These stories are true. Sometimes I will substitute a name, or paraphrase a conversation. I don't want all of my friends and family to be mad at me.

I debated with myself often about sharing several pieces because they're very personal. Ultimately I knew readers are smart people. They can sense a withhold. To be authentic I must be willing to be open and vulnerable. I admit, I'm a flawed creature with good intent. I truly want to add value to the lives of others.

SQUARE LIFE

I grew up in a house with fifteen people including a bunch of kids, siblings and cousins, grandparents, aunts, uncles and various family friends who were going through a rough patch at any given time. My cousins are my brothers and sisters. I figure if you eat together, sleep in the same bed, wear each other's cloths and take baths with these people, they're more like your siblings. There was a lot of love and no money.

We had great home training. *"Please, thank you, excuse me,"* on and on, how to eat with a knife and fork, etc. *"Don't embarrass your family."* We got this drill every day. You just simply can't have a bunch of unruly kids in the house. My family has always been very well respected in the community.

By the time I was in my mid-teens, I was in full rebellion. I smoked weed, hung out in the pool room, wore a big brimmed fedora, and had long hair, past my shoulders. I was the kind of guy that if I went over to a girl's house I could sense her mother saying, *"No. not this guy."* And she would have been right. I was one of those naughty but nice guys with a zest for life. I was willing to take the punishment when I got home but in the meantime, I wanted to go everywhere and try everything at least once. So that's just what I did.

Between nineteen and twenty, I was a pallbearer at three of my friend's funerals. That's right, three in one year. All were drug or alcohol related. These were my good friends that I had known forever. We were together before we thought taking a bath or combing our hair was important, before we liked girls. We could go to each other's homes and eat when the other wasn't even there. I had saved the third ones' life when we were 10 years old. His death was incredibly painful for me. His funeral was on my 21st birthday.

After the funeral everyone went to the house for the repast to eat and reflect. There had to be over 100 people. I was standing quietly against the wall when all of a sudden I blanked. No one was there. I saw three drops falling with the third one landing right between my feet. Blood drops. From Gods' mouth to my ear came these words, *"Straighten up your life or you're the next one in line!"* Then everyone was back. It only took an instant, but I got the message loud and clear.

My heroes have always been bad guys, Ming the Merciless, Biggie Rat, Scrooge, Odd Job, Darth Vader, and the Wicked Witch of the West. I still love her. But right then, all I could think about was, *"I don't want to be dead or in jail when I'm twenty-one. Who's not going to jail? Who's not getting killed? Whose parents are proud of them? The square boys!"*

You know these guys with their cotton Dockers and Polo sweaters who played on the football or baseball team but never played hooky, protested anything, or got kicked out of anywhere; the ones who had the same girlfriend for two or three years; the ones who always look up or look down at people; the ones who went to the Cotillion/Debutante dance; the ones who thought the brown paper bag test was funny; the ones whose parents told them to stay away from my side of town; the ones who always played it safe and expected you to care what they thought; the ones who everybody else is compared to; and certainly girls of the same description and disposition. We all know them, the *'Pretty People.'* But they weren't going to jail. They weren't getting killed. Their parents were proud of them - mine weren't.

Before I took one step, I made a solemn pledge to myself out loud, *"I'm going to lead a 'Square Life' like the square boys."*

I came from a good family. I knew how to do it. Things had to change. As I was leaving, I turned around and looked right into his mother's face. We hugged long and hard. She wiped my tears away. Despite her tremendous loss, I could feel her love and compassion for me. I'll never forget that look. Three days later I moved eight hundred miles away to get in school. It was early

September. I hadn't even applied, but I just wanted to be anywhere but home. I had to go.

*****

I enrolled in college and moved on campus. I hated the dorm. It was a tiny room with another guy, and we had to share a communal bathroom with 30 other guys. I felt like I had nothing in common with these people. I had been on my own taking care of myself for a few years by then with a nice apartment, a car, two ten speed bicycles, and a $20,000 income.

After the fourth day I called my mom and told her I was moving off campus. She told me she wanted me to stay, that it would get better.

Then my father got on the phone and said, *"If you move off campus I'm cutting the water off"* as if he had helped me in the first place.

I said, *"What water?"* click. I hung up. I left home at eighteen and hadn't asked them for anything for years. I got my stuff and left.

I paid my way through that first year of college shooting pool. I was a student by day and hustler by night. I made a deal with a guy at a gas station that I would clean both bathrooms every night if he would let me park my car there and sleep. He was lazy anyway. But to me it was a nice clean bathroom with hot and cold running water, and electricity. There were lights so I could study at night, and a safe place to sleep. I had one jacket, four shirts, and three pair of pants. Every night I would clean the hell out of those bathrooms. Then wash a shirt and a pair of pants, lay a towel on the floor, iron them, wash the towel, and go to school the next day.

I had a full load of classes but only one book. I wrote my name in bold magic marker on the paper side of it. Someone stole it the first week. I also had a syllabus. I would get to the library at seven in the morning. Seeing what the next lesson was, I would read the one chapter in three different books on the topic of the lesson for each class. Then go to class ready.

One day I went to the student snack bar around lunch time. There were maybe forty people in there. As I was leaving, two tables from the door, I saw my book and picked it up.

The young man sitting there said, *"That's my book."*

I said, *"No, this is my book. This is my name. This is my book."*

He said, *"I bought that book."*

"Then you need to get your money back from the thief who stole it from me."

He stood up abruptly with the table between us and said, *"I'm a ..."* as he loudly proclaimed his fraternity affiliation, two more young men stood up.

I started backing towards the door scanning the room for any more of his friends and said, *"I'm a long way from home. I don't have any friends. I've buried three of my best friends this year, the last one about a month ago. I came down here to straighten up my life and this book is a part of that. But I figure my life is on a short leash anyway. I was the next one in line. Everybody doesn't get a happy ending. So I'm prepared to call my mom and tell her I'm not going to graduate from college. I got expelled for a book. They carried me out on a stretcher. Or they carried me out in handcuffs and I'm about to do some time. Either way I'm okay with it. So before we jump off this cliff, before you involve your friends, you should decide how much my stolen book means to you. And decide if you're prepared to call your mom too."*

We locked eyes. The whole room was silent. With my back to the door and book in hand I said, *"I hope we can both get to graduation."* I nodded at him and he at me as a gesture of respect. Then I departed.

I pulled a 3.8 Grade Point Average (GPA) that term.

My top priority was keeping gas in my car. Without gas I was truly homeless. With gas I had mobility and a roof over my head. Understand, there is homeless and crazy, homeless and sick, homeless and alcoholic or drug addicted, homeless and handicapped, homeless with children, homeless and hopeless. I was none of those things. I had a car and a purpose. That alone elevated me to the 'elite homeless.' My second priority was paying tuition. I was determined go to school. My third priority was getting something to eat. I lost 30 pounds in 45 days, broke, 800 miles from home, but I didn't care about that. I was meeting my objectives.

I had one class three days a week at a different college about a mile and a half away. I would walk because it was impossible to find a parking space over there anyway. The fastest route was to walk through a rough neighborhood called 'The Bottom.' On the way was a greasy little hole-in-the-wall, storefront chicken joint with three or four ladies working hard. You could get a good size chicken breast and two pieces of bread for one dollar. It was always sweat-through-your-clothes hot in there. I would come in, smile, politely say hello to the ladies, and place the same order every time. It's what I could afford. On those days, that would be my only meal for the day. After a month or so, I would find two chicken breasts in my bag. It may have been a small gesture to them, but it sure was a big deal to me. They were always busy so we never talked. I don't know which one of those ladies was looking out for me. I certainly wasn't going to tell it and give her away. Those ladies were angels to me. In the grip of hunger, I found angels. You never know where angels dwell. I'm thankful. God bless those kind-hearted ladies in 'The Bottom.'

After school I would put on my street gear: slacks, shined shoes, long sleeved pin-point button down oxford shirt, three inch brim, and my 'day by day' hustler's jacket. When I put on my 'day by day' hustler's jacket it was time to get paid. Then I'd go to various poolhalls around the city. I had a razor sharp eye, a steady hand, and ice water in my veins.

There were all kinds of people on the street. There were players, pimps and working girls, gamblers, thieves and robbers, con men, safe crackers, drug dealers, dope fiends, runaways, and throwaways of every description. What I liked about them was they were not in judgment all the time. At school, in the square world, the students and staff were cliquish and very judgmental. It was all about where you're from, who your friends are, what fraternity you're in, what your major is, what your GPA is, if you were in the band, or played sports, etc. On the street it was about, *'Are you game or are you lame?'* That's it. I was down for my full-tilt hustle all the time. I was game. I got paid. I got respect.

There was a kind of hierarchy out there. At the top were players, pimps, good working girls who kept themselves up, safe crackers, gamblers who never welched on a bet and whose marker was always good, burglars who only stole from businesses but not individuals, and con men who left good people alone. They would take the greedy but not the gullible. These were skilled positions. These were professionals, craftsman, and artisans of sorts.

On the lower tier were drug dealers because they attracted a lot of traffic from riff raff and the police. Although if they weren't strung out, and could stay out of jail, could get respect   because they had money. There were thieves and stick-up men who would break into your home or put a gun in your face, unkempt working girls, and dope fiends. Most people would try to help the young and the runaways or just leave them alone instead of taking them fast. They got a pass.

One night I ran across a street guy I casually knew and we were headed for the same place walking. He said, *"Let's cut down this way."*

"No man, that's not a good idea. The stick-up man hangs out down there."

He assured me it would be okay, but I wasn't going for it. Then he said, *"Don't sweat it bro. You'll be alright. I am the stick-up man."*

We got a real good laugh out of that. I felt totally secure with him. It's great to be on the good side of the stick-up man. So we went.

There was another guy, Terry, who was a player extraordinaire. He was dedicated to the game. He could do it all. He was six feet tall with dark smooth skin and every hair in place. His teeth were so white they would glisten when he smiled. His dress was impeccable. He was street clean all the time in his walking suits, or Italian knit shirts, alligator shoes, gabardine pants, and suede or leather coats with a fur collar. Terry might easily have $2000 on his back and possibly a bankroll to match at any given time. He was a generalist. He was a gambler, a small-scale drug dealer, only when he could make a fast buck but not as a matter of course. He could talk trash at a mile a minute with a million one-liners, and he loved to laugh. He had several female friends, most of who could help him out in time of need, and one true love, El. He and El had been together since they were kids. They lived together and had a baby of their own.

As it was told on firsthand account, one morning Terry came home as the sun was rising about 6:00 a.m. This was not particularly unusual. This is Terry we're talking about. But this particular morning El met him at the door with a pistol in her hand. *"Where you been? You been out with one of them bitches. You got a baby at home."*

He told her, *"Don't be quizzing me. I'm taking care of my business."*

She shot him once, BANG, and then again, BANG, at point-blank range. He grabbed his chest. And as he slowly slid down the wall with the essence of life dripping onto the porch, and his mortal life in peril, he looked up at El and said, *"Is the macaroni gonna go down like this?"* Right then, Terry secured his place in player lore. He became a legend that day.

Four pimps, Bobby, Top Dog, Funlovin, and Easylivin took me under their wing. They would school me in the game. They wanted to give me something, a trade to fall back on in case college didn't work out, like a carpenter would do. It was not until later that I realized they purposely kept most of the real drama away from me. They didn't want me to catch a case. They protected me as best they could. They had rules, ethics, and principles, a code they lived by. They had honor and a kind of morality, not the same as acceptable by what we would call 'decent' people, but nonetheless. They were professionals. There was order in their world. They had Lincoln Town cars, Fleetwood Broughams, the finest clothes and jewelry.

The women were well groomed, clothed, and housed. All of the children were accepted as family. It didn't matter who the real father was. For some of them the children going to good schools, playing sports, having a good vocabulary, and being well rounded meant a lot to them. They wanted their children to be able to cross over into the square world. That was important. Like parents everywhere, good grades, and seeing their children go to college was a measure of accomplishment.

It's counter-intuitive but the position of the women was held in a kind of honored place. They were taken in, protected, and thought of like family. They could choose to stay or leave and take up with someone else. They were respected for their work and their skills. In fact, they validated the pimp's leadership in an alternative worldly kind of way.

I know this is a stretch from a square world point of view. I don't pretend to justify this kind of working relationship for any reason. It is base, immoral, sometimes brutal, and leaves emotional scars for all concerned. People will surely judge me for writing this. But it did make an odd kind of sense to them and to me. These guys were at the 'top of their game.' They got paid. They got respect in the 'street' community.

The four pimps were committed to their craft. They saw potential in me. They had 'street walking' and 'gentleman's club' women working for them. But they felt that because I was well-spoken, clean cut, educated, and game, I could take it to the next level by getting 'call girl' women and 'high-class society' women working for me. They would tell me, *"When you get chose you can maintain a gentleman's front and ride it out until the bitter end."* (Big laughs everywhere.) It was a gallows kind of humor because for most people on the street who stay out there too long, there really is a bitter end.

Thanksgiving rolled around. All of the students had gone home or somewhere. I had been thinking all morning long about our big family dinner with turkey, dressing, and all the fixings. Finally, about one o'clock, I decided I was going to find a Thanksgiving dinner.

I ended up at a big church in a long line full of down and outers. There were the shell-shocked war veterans, homeless mothers with their little children, grocery cart pushers, and those with all of their worldly possessions on their backs. And there I was with shirt, slacks, and shined shoes thinking, *"Is it worth it? I don't belong here."* But I was homeless and hungry too. So I went to the front of the line and asked the lady at the door if I could help. I told her I was a student a long way from home. I showed her my student ID and my out of state driver's License.

She smiled and let me in saying, *"What a nice young man."*

For the rest of the afternoon, I served, swept floors, bussed tables, cleaned up, washed dishes, and helped the people feel welcomed. I felt incredibly good about what I was doing. It was the least I could do. Every time I looked at those being served I knew that *'There, but for the grace of God, go I.'* That was the best Thanksgiving I've ever had. By five o'clock we were done serving. Now we could eat. I had a huge plate in front of me. I was happy.

One of the ladies who also had been working, the one that let me in initially, sat down next to me to eat. She asked, *"Where do you live?"*

I just looked at her.

She asked if I heard her.

"Yes ma'am. I heard you. I don't live anywhere. I live in my car."

"You mean to tell me you're homeless?"

"No ma'am. I live in my car. My car is my home."

"Didn't you tell me you were in college? How can you be in school?"

"My car doesn't stop me from learning ma'am. It takes me to school every day."

She called out to another lady who came over right away and told her what I had said. Without saying a word, the lady wrote a note and gave it to me. It simply read, *"Call me at this number Monday morning."* I held on tightly to that number. I knew it was something special. I called on Monday.

She said, *"Write down this address. Get there. It'll be okay."* Those were the only words she ever said to me. I never saw her again. Later that day I had my own big furnished room in a house with two other boarders in a nice neighborhood, paid up for three months. Both of those ladies were angels. In the midst of human misery, again I found angels. We never know where angels dwell. The only way I could repay their kindness is to pass it on.

For the next three weeks I hustled hard to make enough money to get home for Christmas, but I had to pay tuition before they let me take finals. My bankroll was depleted.

One night at about ten o'clock when I was on my way in, I saw a professional girl on the corner. It was pouring down raining. For some unknown reason I felt compassion for her. I had on my street gear. I stopped. After she understood I didn't want a date I said, *"Why don't you get out of the rain? There are no cars out here. You're not making any money and you could catch pneumonia. I'll give you a ride if you need one."*

She refused.

I said, *"Okay. I'm going to get something to eat. If you want to come, I'll buy."* She hopped in. We went to a little all-night diner, ordered, and began to talk.

She opened up to me. I don't know why but she told me her life story and I listened. She was a very good-looking woman, articulate, smart and funny, a really interesting person. She easily could have been a nurse or a teacher. After a while the rain let up. I had to go. The library opens at 7:00 a.m. Then she looked at me very seriously. I knew she had something she wanted to say but wasn't sure how to say it. I just hoped she wasn't going to ask me for anything.

She said, *"Have you ever thought about pimpin'?"*

I said, *"Yes I have, quite a bit."*

She said, *"I'm choosing you. I'll work for you. I'll teach you everything. I'll take good care of you."*

In that moment, she was sweetest girl in the whole world. She touched my heart. I loved her for that. I really had to think about it. For me, this was like graduation. My street associates would have been proud of me. Men normally find women and take the right of approach. Women take the right of refusal. So, no matter how much game you have, if you don't get chose, you're not pimping. If you don't get chose, you don't have a girlfriend. There are a lot of things you can take from a woman but her heart must be given by choice. From the church house, to the board room, in the square world or on the street, whatever world you live in, women always do the choosing. I got chose.

I told her how honored I felt. I meant it. I knew it was a big deal. But then told her how I had made a pledge to lead a square life. I was in school and for now just trying to make enough money to get home for Christmas. She seemed a little disappointed yet I could tell how she admired my decision to stay in the square world. It was time to go. I offered her ride to anywhere she wanted. She asked me to take her back to where I found her. As I dropped her off she said she hoped I could get home for Christmas. It was done.

I thought about our encounter all the way back to my room. Upon arriving, I got ready for bed. I washed up, hung up my clothes, and just before turning out the light, I checked my pockets. To my total surprise she had slipped two hundred dollars into the pocket of my day-by-day hustler's jacket closest to where she had been sitting. I was going home for Christmas. She was an angel. In the midst of immorality, again, I found an angel. We never know where angels dwell. Until this day, I still have a soft spot in my heart for the professional girls out there.

It is not my intent to glorify street life. It's a hard, perilous, and possibly dangerous way to go. By my junior and senior years the school environment became more hospitable to me. I certainly encourage both young and older people to be lifelong learners. I was committed to my education from the start. My attendance and grades were outstanding, and I personally paid my own way – in cash. I simply didn't know and no one ever told me that grants, and academic scholarships could be for me. However, when I was going from hand to mouth for food, clothing, and shelter on a daily basis, it was the kindness of strangers in the street and larger community who accepted, supported, and embraced me. So I speak of them with affection and give them their due respect. Those in the academic community did not. It's no wonder why so many of our young Black and Latino men turn to the streets.

As you know, I paid my first year of college shooting pool. My second year I rented a carpet cleaner, *three carpets, $35 dollars*. My junior year I painted addresses on curbs for $7 a pop. My senior year I had a landscaping business. I graduated from college with honors, National Deans List, offers for grad school, and zero debt. I went on to own several businesses over time.

*****

Twenty years later on a snowy Christmas Eve, I knocked on the door of my third friends' mother. I hadn't seen her since the funeral. We hugged long and hard but this time it was filled with joy. I told her how the loss of her son had changed my life and about the pledge I had made to lead a square life. She was proud of me. I was her boy too. We were both comforted by the outcome. Their family will always be branded into the fabric of my life.

I also saw Terry (the player extraordinaire) at The Million Man March in Washington DC in 1995. He and El were still together with two more kids and a grandchild on the way. He looked good with a touch of grey. He was a hard working Christian man.

In 2007 I saw Top Dog in Chicago at a backyard barbecue. He was one of the pimps who had taken me under their wing. He was physically fit, street clean, and as mentally sharp as ever. Time had been kind to him. He had always been the most clear and contemplative about the code. Now he's the owner of a few three-flats on the west side. He cleaned up his money on the real estate tip. He had three grown children, a younger wife/companion (I didn't ask) and a ten-year old little girl who just adored him. She sat on his lap and loved hearing about how good he had treated me when I was young, far from home, and needed a friend. Without getting into detail, it was gratifying for me to let him know that I appreciated what he had done for me. I'm sure he liked that his daughter heard it. I may have poured it on a little thick but so what. If I could make him a hero in his daughter's eyes I was happy to do it. He was maintaining a gentleman's front and riding it out… He seemed wise and content.

I still feel like I live on the outskirts of polite society, close enough to get to it but not necessarily feeling a need to be there. The *"Pretty People"* accept me now with varying degrees of comfort. I know them. Some actually want to meet me or hang out together. The zest for life has never left me. I still wear a big brimmed fedora although I'm clean shaven with short hair now. I look like them. I go where they go, and sometimes where they're too cautious to go. I might say things that they may be too nice or politically correct to say. I understand why they still scratch their heads and look at me sideways. I'm not quite an exact fit. I choose to be one of the good guys yet I treasure what I got on the street, the ability to appreciate the good in people whatever their condition may be. The concept of better than or less than other people just doesn't work for me. I don't have to cast a shadow on others for the sun to shine on me. I learned to keep my judgment out of the way.

You can ignore your home training but it doesn't go away. We all still hear our upbringing in our heads. I guess the child in all of us still wants our parents' approval. Although it took many years, I was told that my parents were very proud of me. I didn't know that. It was good to hear. A few years ago I bought my family home. It's the very place I couldn't wait to get away from. I love this place. I have become a well-respected, contributing member of our community. And I continue to lead a square life.

Book One

Start Where You Are

See it. Speak it. Claim your power.

Faith is the catalyst, the manifesting agent.

The Facts Don't Matter

<u>EVICTION: Resident Must Evacuate The Premises Immediately!!!</u>

It was a huge, bright orange, glow-in-the dark poster pasted on the front door. And then they put all my worldly possessions on the curb- just sprawled out there in a big pile with total disregard for quality or sentimental value. The neighborhood was a nice tucked-away little subdivision about fifteen years old. Every house was one of four styles, each with a six foot grudge fence in the back yard. If you didn't have a need to be in there, you would never notice it from the main road. It was old enough for some kids to have grown up there and call it home but not yet old enough to have big trees. It made me feel about two inches tall when neighbors slowly rode past looking at my household in all its glory.

To top it off, my wife of one year and her 12 year old son were glaring at me as if to say, *"You horrible man. How could you let this happen? How could you do this to us?"*

I had taken a job that didn't work out twelve hundred miles from home. I was hyper aware of the circumstance, but after a while I felt absolute detachment. It was almost like watching myself in a movie, like it wasn't happening to me. The slow riders, my life on display, and all of the dirty looks meant nothing. It wasn't denial. It just didn't make sense to get absorbed into feeling bad when darkness is coming. We haven't eaten. And we still need a place to sleep. I can feel bad later. At that moment I was thinking in free flow. With my back to the small tree in our currently former front yard, my thoughts went like this:

"I need a job. No I have two jobs now. I'm just not making any money. I don't need another job. I need money. It takes money to make money. Wait a minute. If it takes money to make money, and I don't have any money, can I afford that belief? No. Does that belief serve me? No. Does that belief get me what I want? No."

Then I had this thought:

"It takes ideas to make money. Can I afford that belief? Yes. Hope lives here. This is a belief I can work with."

Then the next thought popped up.

"Okay, what can I do? Where can I go? Who do I know? It's not what you know, it's who you know. Wait a minute. I'm twelve hundred miles from home. If it's not what you know, it's who you know, and I don't know anyone, can I afford that belief? No. Does that belief serve me? No. Does it get me what I want? No.

And finally, this thought:

"When you make up your mind the facts don't matter. When you make a commitment, the right people always show up. Can I afford that belief? Yes. Hope lives here. This is a belief I can work with."

This whole thought process happened in a matter of seconds. It was a great learning experience. Most of us have all kinds of tapes that run continuously in our heads. Be good. Do as you're told. Get a good education. Get a good job, and hundreds more. Most of these tapes serve us well most of the time but when circumstances or the environment changes, we must be willing to change. What was one of the worst days of my life turned out to be one of the best days of my life. On that day I learned to listen to the words that come into my mind or out of my mouth, and examine them.

Now I ask myself, *"Does this belief serve me?"*

If you have beliefs that you are not aware of, you can't change them. On that day I learned how to recognize my beliefs, challenge them, and change them into something that can work.

Faith

What makes you go on when everything says you should stop, when the odds are all against you, when others have called you a fool, turned against you, or have packed up and gone home? What makes you go it alone, give one more effort when you're exhausted, practice in the rain, make one more call? What makes you hold on to that dream, ask one more person, say one more prayer? Ultimately the question is, *"How long can you keep your faith?"* That's the test. That's always the test.

"Faith is the substance of things hoped for and the evidence of things not seen." (Holy Bible)

Faith is the promise. A person with faith can see what cannot be seen by the naked eye. Faith can draw from the invisible. It is the catalyst, the manifesting agent. The greater the faith, the greater the manifest. I had to explore that. I think of hope and desire in the same breath. You must actually want something. I think of the word desire as de-sire: De (French word for 'of'); and Sire (sire is word for 'Father'). De Sire is 'Of the Father.' It is the starting point.

Substance is something real. It has a presence. It exists. And evidence is the indication and proof that the substance (the thing) does, in fact, exist. It is no longer speculation when you have evidence. Your faith is the substance and the evidence.

So let us say you're looking for deer in the woods. The evidence is their tracks that show you they have been through here. They also scrape their horns on trunks of trees which leave marks. They nibble on certain types of plants and leave droppings along the way which is more evidence that they could be around. You still haven't seen them but the evidence shows you they might be nearby. So you continue to look. But first you must hope to find them and believe it will be done.

Faith is like that. It is the substance of things hoped for. You must desire something. Speak it. Claim it. *"People receive not because they ask not"* (Quote unknown.) You must believe it can come to pass.

Then do something. You must move your feet. Otherwise it's just talk. You must take action in that direction. Action is the physical manifestation of your faith. Action is the glue that binds your destiny to your dreams. *"Faith without works is dead."* (Holy Bible.) I tend to look at where people put their time, money, and effort. It shows me what they believe in. It tells me where their faith is.

So the test is always: How long can you keep your faith? How long can you fall into rat holes and scrape up your shins? How long can you bang your head on some glass ceiling? How long can you trip over hurdles, get detoured, find another way? How long can you go without permission, appreciation, validation, and sometimes without compensation, and still feel like your hope will be fulfilled? How long can you hold on tightly to that dream? How long can you leave room for miracles in your life?
How long can you keep your faith?

Courage

Courage = commitment + doubt + action + naïveté'

Commitment is when there is no turning back. It is doing what you say you will do long after the feeling you said it in is gone. When you stand at the altar and say *"I do,"* that is commitment. At three months and one day a woman says *"I will have this baby,"* that is commitment. When a soldier picks up his weapon and goes into battle, that is commitment. You get the point.

Doubt is fear or great concern of an unfavorable outcome. You will hear yourself saying things like, *"I could lose everything." "I could look like a fool." "This could literally cost me my life."* This is doubt.

Action with purpose is the physical manifestation of your faith.

So what happens when you take action? You get a reaction, right? Then what happens when you take another action? Something happens again. If you continue to take action in succession, you begin to gain momentum or accelerating acceleration. This propels you to the threshold more quickly than you would imagine.

The *threshold* is the point of entry or the point of beginning to something new or different. A newlywed husband carries his wife across the threshold of their home into a new life. It is the point where you must make a decision to stay out or go through. You must change course or continue. It is a step into the unknown. It is a leap of faith. You alone must choose.

This is also the point where the enemy tests your commitment. The threshold is where stuff pops up. Your car breaks down. Someone gets sick. A new job opportunity or a new potential mate comes into your life. It's usually something big that must be considered and can take you off purpose. *This is the point where most people fail.*

The reason most fail here is because they feel that they can stop what they're doing, take care of whatever came up and then get back to the place where they stopped. They feel that they can absorb the distraction. It just doesn't happen. While you were gone, circumstances, finances, and feelings change. Your path takes a different direction. Time marches on. In essence, you failed before you crossed the threshold, before you really started, before you entered into the unknown. You cannot be dragged across. Others should not try to convince you. You must want to come. If you choose not to cross then be clear - you can never get back to that place again.

However, if you step over the threshold your whole world changes. At this point you have committed so much that it would be ridiculous to turn back. It borders on being on a suicidal mission like a soldier who rides alone into battle. You might as well keep on going. Doubt is dispelled. Your purpose becomes clear. Your mind is made up. You begin to trust your instincts and intuition. The words of your critics have less power. You have passed the point of no return.

Naiveté' is a lack of awareness, an innocence of sorts. It's a lack of experience or informed judgment. It's God's way of protecting you from discouragement. The fact is, if you really knew what it would take for you to get where you wanted to go to reach your objective, you probably wouldn't go.

Courage is not necessarily the absence doubt or fear. It is a willingness to acknowledge your vulnerabilities then still engage the challenge and proceed anyway.

Certain Death

I have always been a seeker. I have always wanted to live the life of my dreams. I have always wanted to be happy, healthy, wealthy, wise, and free.

Sometimes I get stuck in a situation or lifestyle that cannot possibly get me where I want to go even though it might be steady, predictable, and even comfortable. I'm not always sure where the life I want to go is. But I know it's not where I am. I know that to trade what you know, for change and uncertainty, is a hard step to take. Like most people, I am a creature of habit. For me it boils down to this simple formula. It begins with where I am. If I linger here it represents the certain death of my ideal life.

Certain Death < --- > Danger/Opportunity < --- > Freedom/Wealth/Paradise

*****

There was a great and wise Persian ruler who would throw his captive enemies to the lions in a big arena for all to see. But before each person met their gruesome fate the ruler would meet them under the stadium and give them a choice:

"You can go through this door that leads to the arena. Or you can go through the mysterious black door. Choose now."

A vast majority of the time the captives would choose the door to the arena.

On occasion a servant of the ruler would ask, *"Where does the mysterious black door lead to?"*

The ruler replied, *"It's a door that leads outside of the stadium to the street. It leads to freedom. But most would rather choose what they know to what they don't know."*

This story about the ruler was told to me many years ago. (Author unknown)

I made a decision long ago to strive for freedom, wealth, and paradise. Many times I fall short. But I'm always trying to give back, add value, and encourage others in gratitude for the grace God has given me.

Part of this formula was given to me years ago. From whom I do not know. Thank you.

Your True Role

This is a modified quote from Buckminster Fuller:

"Your true role may forever be obscure to you but you can be assured that if you use your own natural gifts, talents, and experiences for the highest benefit of others, then seemingly inadvertently, but realistically, precessionally, and normally in the nick of time, you will be supported."

There are certainly reasons why many people would not subscribe to this way of being.

1.   A lot of people think what they do on the job or what they studied in school is who they are. *"I am a..."* (fill in the blank). In fact most people have many roles depending on the expanse or intensity of their interests and relationships.

2.   It's very common that people don't know what their *true role* or natural gifts and talents are. I didn't for decades. The problem with gifts and talents is that the person with them may not feel they're special. I suggest that you listen to what people compliment you on or ask you questions about. They may be telling you what you're really good at or what they admire about you. Pay attention to what you do for fun, as a hobby, things you're passionate about, or things you do for free. Pay attention to things that excite you, spur you to action, or seriously annoy you. You might have enough passion for these things to create a better way or to solve a problem.

3.   Also many people don't take the time to reflect on their experiences so they don't consciously see the value in what they've been through. If you don't reflect on your experiences you may miss the lesson.

4.   Is what's happening really inadvertent? Is it coincidental? Is it happenstance? What is your involvement in the ripple? How are you creating, responding, or reacting to the ripple?

The passage suggests that you have a bigger vision or perspective, an openness to work for the greater good. You would have to be somewhat selfless or feel that by helping others you are really helping yourself. It's not always easy to be willing to do what is best for the most people instead of your immediate and personal concerns. I believe that God wants his children to survive. And if we do what is best for the survivability of his children, we will be supported.

Most people bail before they get to the 'nick of time.' They want an insurance policy. They want a guarantee. It is my belief that it is your:

A) Faith: the substance of things hoped for and the evidence of things not seen.

B) Courage: (commitment + doubt + action + naiveté).

C) Commitment: when there's no turning back; doing what you say you will do long after the feeling you said it in is gone.

D) Persistence: the ability to continue or remain.

These things are your guarantee.

Hungry Dog

After six years old, it was my job to take out the trash before I went to bed or mom would wake me up to get it done. It was summer time. The days were long. Mom was looking at flowers in the back yard as I came through. She walked to the alley with me.

At the far end of the alley was a good sized dog. He was up on a garbage can, back down, up on another, back down. Then he'd knock one down. Go through it. Then back up on another. It only took a minute or two for him to inspect five or six cans as we watched from a distance.

Mom said, *"Do you see that dog down there?"*

"Yes ma'am." (She was big on manners).

She said, *"He doesn't exactly know what he's looking for but he has an idea and he knows it when he finds it. He's not desperate. He's deliberate."* She bent down putting both hands on her knees and started looking from side to side. Then she pointed at me and said, *"That's how you are. You're curious. You watch. You test the limits for possibilities. You marvel at little things. You have a hustler's heart."*

Most people, including myself, prefer a relatively high degree of certainty and expectation in our lives. We want to eat every day, get bills paid, feel that somebody cares about us somewhere, and have an idea of what the future may hold for us. We go to school, work, or have a routine that we become comfortable with regardless of whether we like it or not; sometimes, regardless of whether or not it even works for us, as long as it's predictable. Many will sacrifice great amounts of time, blood, and treasure to maintain this level of certainty.

Yet sometimes, with or without any fault of our own, there are times in our lives when circumstances become quite unpredictable. For many people this causes great stress, even fear. It can be hard to make the shift.

When uncertainty comes upon me I tend to get more creative. It's not an emotional place. It's an intuitive place, a place of anticipation. My thought process becomes linear: *"What happened before that? What happens after that?"* My thought process becomes lateral: *"How can this (whatever it is) apply or transfer to another situation?"*

You become keenly aware of what is, and what could be (always within the borders of what is legal, moral, and ethical). You feel alive. You can see potential in the smallest openings. You don't care what people think. You cut back, put aside or dismiss anything that doesn't register. You seem to know what you don't want or need. You're in search mode, watching and checking everything.

I pray that God put the right people in my path and shows me the next step. I don't know exactly where I'm looking, how to get there, or what it will take. But I do have an idea of an outcome. I know it when I find something useful. I feel like I'm on the verge of something big. My prime intent is to be ready when it reveals itself. There's nothing like being hungry to make you think better and explore your options. I call these times the 'Hungry Dog' times.

It's the place where uncertainty gets actively engaged with hope and anticipation. It's not desperate. It's deliberate.

Five Hundred Dollars

I had just quit my job three weeks before and had $25 in my pocket. Now the rent is due in five days. I knew a lot about landscaping but I didn't know anything about how to run a business. I didn't have any business cards but I did have about fifty 3x5 index cards with my contact info and a catchy phrase about what a great landscaper I was (Earthshaper Landscaper...Real Live Landscaper... Professional Horticulturist...). I had just made them up right after my wife asked if I had the rent money. The rent was $400. The night before I'd said, *"Don't worry about it."*. Now it's four o'clock in the morning and I'm sitting in my raggedy pickup truck named Buzz (short for buzzard trucking) in the driveway like I really had somewhere to go. I start it up and pull off slowly into the darkness.

"Five hundred dollars; Five hundred dollars," is what I was saying out loud over and over again. By seven o'clock I had said it over a thousand times, literally. I was no longer hoping, I was looking for my money and I knew it was out there. I couldn't go home without it. I had reached resolve.

I had already stopped at several garden centers, nurseries, and outdoor plant marts. *"I'm with Earthshaper Landscaper and I'm a real live landscaper. Do you have any work for me?"*

"We're not hiring."

"I'm not looking for a job. I'm looking for some work. Do you have any work for me?"

"No."

This must have happened fifteen times. It didn't matter. I was on full scan for an opportunity with the intent to get one. *"Five hundred dollars; Five hundred dollars,"* is what I kept on saying. By about 9:30 I came across a place that sold sod grass and pulled in.

There were about a dozen guys in the construction shed when I came in. *"I'm with Earthshaper Landscaper and I'm a real live landscaper..."* I handed the owner one of my index cards.

He read it and said, *"Oh great, another idiot with a degree."* We all got a good laugh. He quizzed me about soils, lawn chemicals, watering practices, etc. all of which I was able to answer. After toying with me for 15 minutes I could tell he liked me but he just didn't have anything for me to do.

I wished him well and went to my truck. Then I noticed a convenience store next door. I went in and bought a 12 pack of beer, not for myself, for them. I went right back, put it on the counter and went back to my truck. As I was about to pull out I heard someone whistle and turned around to look. It was the owner waving me back.

"You ever laid grass?"

"Yeah"

"I got six pallets need layin' by this afternoon. Want it?"

"Yeah, how much do I charge?"

"Fifty dollars a pallet."

"How long should it take?" He knew I was green.

"If you wiggle fast, you get through fast just like when you're with your girlfriend."

He gave me the address where he would drop it. On the way I bought a pocket knife, a machete to cut the sod, and a book called All About Lawns. I made three hundred dollars that day.

At four o'clock the next morning I started up Buzz and pulled off slowly into the darkness   saying, *"Five hundred dollars; Five hundred dollars."*

It was still early when I rolled up to the construction trailer of a huge builder/developer in a brand new subdivision with the roads marked out but still unpaved. Front-end loaders were still knocking down trees. There were six beautiful model homes and about fifteen homes in varying stages of completion but none occupied.

"I'm with Earthshaper Landscaper and I'm a real live landscaper…" An old grizzled, unshaven site manager looked me up and down over his glasses without lifting his head.

"You got a lotta' nerve coming in here like this. Why should I hire you?"

"Hire me because you would be hard pressed to just stumble across a real live landscaper like me. Plus I'm hungry. You would rather have a hungry man than a greedy man any day."

"Do you cut grass?"

"Yeah."

He told me where to go and come back with a price. It was a big lawn but no big deal.

"Thirty five dollars."

I didn't have a lawnmower so I rented one for fifteen dollars, got it done perfectly like they do on baseball diamonds, and took the lawnmower back.

"What else you got for me?"

"Have you ever done a rake out?" That's when they dump a few truckloads of topsoil in a yard but it needs to be spread out and graded.

"Seventy five dollars."

"Do it."

I had to buy a wheelbarrow. I had never done a rake out but I knew water seeks level and has to drain away. I put my face on the ground and asked myself, *"If I was water where would go?"* This one took most of the day. When I finished it was beautiful. Not even a foot print could be found on it when I left.

He checked it out. *"Pretty good."* he said. I had made over a hundred dollars that day.

At four o'clock the next morning the rent is due in two days and I'm still over $100 short. I started up Buzz and pulled off slowly into the darkness saying, *"Five hundred dollars; Five hundred dollars."*

The sun was just rising when I rolled up to that same construction shack and the same old grizzled site manager looked up at me over his glasses.

"I'm with Earthshaper Landscaper and I'm a real live landscaper. What kind of work do you have for me?" He smiled this time.

"You ever laid grass?"

With a big smile on my face I said, *"Yeah, I'm a real live landscaper."*

"Go to this address and talk to this manager. He's got a truckload of grass needs layin'. Get out of here."

Enroute I had to get on the expressway. Just ahead of me I saw a young guy dart across six lanes on foot. I pulled over and beckoned to him. *"You looking for work?"*

"Yeah."

"You ready right now?"

"Yeah, my name is Mike."

"Let's go."

He hopped in and we went to the job site where there was an 18 wheeler loaded to the gills with grass.

Mike said, *"That's lot of grass. How long do you think it will take?"*

I told him, *"If you wiggle fast you get through fast, just like when you're with your girlfriend."*

The site manager, Carl, greeted me and told me he was in a pinch to get this done. He was a week behind, over budget, and the buyer was doing an inspection the next day. He asked how much I would charge.

"Normally I charge fifty dollars a pallet but I don't want to kick a man when he's down. Forty dollars a pallet will do this time. That will save you a couple hundred bucks. What I want from you is to call me first for any landscaping work."

"Deal." We shook on it.

When no one was looking I pulled out my book, <u>All About Lawns</u> to review the process. Then Mike and I got busy. The only way I knew to do the job was textbook style. Our work was impeccable. Carl was impressed and told me we saved his butt. I made over seven hundred dollars that day and paid the rent.

Both Earthshaper Landscaper and Buzz are now distant, pleasant memories. One thing still remains. When times get tight and I'm looking for answers, I start up my ride at four o'clock in the morning and pull off slowly into the darkness.

Mistakes

Mistakes are divinely sent for us to learn.

You get on the bike. You fall off. You get back on the bike. You fall off and scrape your knee. You kick the bike. Your friends laugh. It's embarrassing and it hurts. But the pain of not riding and joining your friends, not to speak of the freedom it could give you, is worse than that of your scraped up knee. You get back on the bike. You wobble, wobble. *"Hey, I can ride!"* You're excited. Then you run into the bushes or a parked car. How do you turn or stop this thing? You stumble forward. We've all seen babies learning to walk. How many times are they willing to fall down? The next thing you know, they can run. We learn to drive with both hands on the wheel paying full attention. Later you have the radio going, eating something, and ladies putting their makeup on. That's how we learn.

If you're afraid to make mistakes you're already making a mistake. Yet it's an understandable fear. In major areas of our lives, we get penalized for making them. It starts sooner than any of us can remember. Don't touch this. Don't eat that. You could poke somebody's eye out. Then you go to school. Get good grades. If you don't, all kinds of bad things can happen in your future. You go to worship. If you do whatever you like, you're going straight to hell in a hand basket. You go to work. You will be fired if you … Fill in the blank. It's amazing people get anything done. Most of these fears have some reasonable basis. They either make sense or we believe the warnings of people who care about us. In fact, most of the warnings are valid. Yes, you really could get hurt, flunk out, get fired, or go to hell in a hand basket.

It is my belief that God wants us to have what we want as long as it does not step on the rights of other people and we come and ask according to His word. I believe that so long as we want things that improve the quality of life on the planet, he's okay with that. Mistakes are God's way of confronting us with what we don't know. Mistakes make us aware of what we need to know next.

That's the beauty of them. They can act as a guide to our future success. Many times opportunity is veiled in adversity. They give you a clue and a problem to solve. Sometimes I think of God as an action figure who sees what you need and then drops a crumb in your path to find, like in Hansel and Gretel, so you can find your way home. The catch is you have to keep looking for the crumbs. Many times people fail because they stop looking for the crumbs. They give up.

Mistakes also force us to make a decision. It is important to pick our battles. Every challenge is not worth the fight. Indeed, most are not. We should ask ourselves if it's worth it. Will I try again? I believe most people waste their mistakes. They say, *"I'll never do that again."* They walk away and have a chicken-little warning for anyone else who would even think about trying the same thing. They don't ask, *"How could I do it differently? What is the lesson? What corrections can be made?"* They just stop looking for the crumbs.

How do we turn a mistake into a benefit? All of us have an internal gauge that tells us what we can live with or cannot live without and, if and when that line has been crossed. Once crossed, something has to change. You become a seeker. You have to want something different bad enough to do something about it. Desire is the starting point of all achievement. (Nepolian Hill) You have to be fundamentally dissatisfied with the current set of circumstances. You have to recognize a problem.

A lot of people stop right there because they think they are the problem or they blame others for their mistakes. All kinds of things come up for them. They think other people must have known what they were doing. Others are smarter. It's a personal problem. Maybe so, but it might be a structural problem, a glitch in the system, an oversight or an incomplete process. It happens every day, all the time. Maybe you see what others don't. It would be wise for employers to watch and listen to new people because they may have a fresh perspective or solve a problem differently than the norm. You need to have a curiosity about what could make it better. Then make a commitment to solve the problem. Make a correction. You have to look for the crumbs. *"A problem once recognized becomes yours to solve."* (Buckminster Fuller).

It is my belief that God gives us good and bad sticky notes. If you're getting mostly good notes then keep doing what you're doing. Great relationships, money in the bank, promotions on the job, and good grades are examples of good notes. If not, then a correction is in order.

Bad sticky notes come in all forms too. Fender benders and traffic tickets, arguments and misunderstandings, a cold or some kind of illness, less than satisfactory grades or job reviews, a low credit score, and debt are all examples of bad notes. If you don't pay attention to the bad notes and make constant and relatively quick corrections, then God sends the earthquake to shake things up. Getting fired, flunking out, bankruptcy, and divorce are examples of the earthquake. Large slow corrections are the hallmark of big mistakes. I personally try not to penalize others or beat myself up over making mistakes. We're human. Everyone makes them. I will drop the hammer on someone for a cover up or for repeatedly making the same mistake and not correcting quickly.

Babies are born with the natural fear of loud noises and the fear of falling. Adults have a natural fear of rejection, fear of a stranger coming toward them, and a fear of the unknown. When you decide to solve the problem, you must take a leap into the unknown. Now you must be willing to make another mistake, walk alone, meet massive resistance, be ridiculed, or even face persecution. Even though you know where you want to end up, you must be willing to suspend your beliefs and judgments about how things are supposed to be and just look at the evidence. What actually happens? What really works? Sometimes it's by trial and error. Other times you follow your intuition to see where it takes you. You feel like you're on your own. There's no one out there. It becomes your responsibility to find the answers. This is where danger and opportunity hold hands. You are now in the process of discovery. You're at the edge of what you know. This is where learning and growth occur.

35

In order to make corrections you must first get past your own personal degree of misery. Get over yourself. Ouch! Now move on. The world doesn't revolve around you. Then you must reflect. Wisdom comes from experience plus reflection. Wisdom dictates that you reflect on your experiences in order to get the lessons. Smart people learn from their mistakes. Geniuses learn from other peoples' mistakes. I want failure to find easier targets than me.

Sometimes God's grace is upon us and we get an insight, a revelation, a notion that shows us exactly how to proceed. It's like the blinders being lifted and we can see what was in front of us all the time. It's a gift.

Mistakes are extremely valuable. The big mistakes represent the exclamation points in our lives. There are many things that can hurt you in the world but mistakes imply that there was something that we could have done differently. Many times they are self-inflicted. That's why they hurt so badly. They are turning points where we have to make a choice. We can say, *"I'll never do that again"* or we can reflect to review the experience. Find the lessons. Then continue to look for the crumbs.

Book Two

Lessons & Essays

Masters are always striving to improve!

Balance

There were 28 people in the class and all of them were wealthy. More than half of them were millionaires. A lot of them seemed to know each other. Exact Investing was the name of the class held at a resort in Phoenix Arizona 1997. I knew the instructor who had invited me directly. He told me these were his friends and this class gives them a good reason to spend some time together at a nice place with a tax write off, of course.

He said that this class was not really for people like me. It wasn't a matter of ethnicity, education, or social graces. It was a matter of income. All of these people were serious investors meaning that they made at least $200,000 per year, every year, for years and years, and had the resources to hold the conversations that would come up. They call people who go to work every day and get a check on Friday "W2ers." This refers to how *those people* file their taxes.

They have financial issues that most of us don't even know exist. They have a different class of problems. We all know that not having enough money can cause problems. In the same way, having too much money can cause problems as well. This may sound strange but if you listen to them talk for long enough your heart goes out to them. They get a higher class of junk mail. He warned me that I was not the kind of person they normally have much to do with. In other words, I wasn't really rich enough to be there. However, he liked me. He said what he admired about me was, *"You can take it on the chin and get up with your head still held high."* If I was willing to subject myself to that, I could come. I might really learn something.

Who could resist an invitation like that?

For three days we went through drills and skills, exercises and insights, all around the topic of money. It was fascinating. Just like some people are in tune to their bodies or their emotions with great sensitivity, all of these people were in tune with their money. They talk in terms of cash flow, positive or negative net worth, assets and liabilities, shelter, the time-value of money, and return on investment (ROI). They have a relationship with their money. Some people can read a novel and find a connection in their own or someone else's life. These people read financial reports as a point of reference in their own lives. They can read an income statement or a balance sheet and tell you what's going on in your life. They can see with surprising accuracy how you think, what kinds of relationships you have with family and friends, where you live and the likelihood of you reaching the lifestyle you desire.

They refer to their money in an intimate way. They never talk badly about it. Think of it this way. If you have a lady friend but you talk badly about her all the time, is she likely to stay with you? No. In the same way, they never talk badly about their money. They don't say things like 'filthy rich, chump change, or disposable income.' You dispose of a Kleenex, not your income. They have discretionary income. *"Money has ears. It can hear you."*

Again, let's say you have a lady friend and every time she looks up, you're dropping her off. You say you'll call but you may or may not call. You always have something to do like work late, hang out with the boys, go to a baseball game or out of town, without her. Is she likely to stay with you? No. You might be a great guy but you don't pay much attention to her. You don't have any time for her. In the same way, if you spend every dollar you get as soon as it comes in, your money feels like, *"You act like you don't want me around. You say you like me but you just use me and get rid of me as fast as you can. Every time I come by, you don't have time for me."* You didn't spend your money. It left you just like the lady would leave you. *"Money has feelings, a vibe; an energy that can be attracted."* I actively work on maintaining a relationship with my money too. In essence, I want it to know I care.

You cannot make women like you, but you can make yourself more attractive so women want to be with you. The woman of your dreams may actually marry you, have your babies, grow old with you past the point when you're putting your teeth in a glass, and then let you die in her arms. Ideally, what you have to do first is attract her. Second, you must give her reasons to stay - such as marry her. Third, you must help the union grow and expand by having children, combining resources, starting a business, or finding activities you mutually enjoy. From my point of view, the reason there are so many unhappy homes and a high divorce rate is because it's easy to get wrapped up in your daily life and take your eye off the ball in one or more of these areas. Well, money is like that too.

Many of the reasons for financial problems, up to and including bankruptcy are comparable. Some people are good at making money. Some are good at keeping or holding on to the money they have. Others are good at making it grow. Very few are good at all three. Most people take their eye off the ball. Indeed, most Americans think like consumers. Consumers think it's about how much you make so they can buy more stuff. One of the millionaires said, *"If I get a Snickers bar I ask myself, 'Is this consumption or investment?' What's the ROI?"* Everybody laughed.

Money likes people. It wants to be attracted. It wants reasons to stay. It likes having friends and babies and even grand babies. It wants to be cared for. All of the people in this class think and act very much like that. They were the finely tuned professional body builders of finance so to speak. They flex their muscles in their portfolios.

I know that the impression I'm giving of my classmates may appear like they were a bunch of greedy, money grabbing, arrogant, heartless capitalists with no regard for the wellbeing of mankind. This is absolutely not true. Yes, all of them save. Yes, all of them invest. But what may not be apparent is that all of them also tithe their own money in a big way to causes that help thousands of people. They raise millions of dollars for charities, foundations and research of all kinds. They create and invest in businesses that hire hundreds or even thousands of people. They do a lot of good. They know they have been blessed. They work quite hard at choosing where their money can do the most good for other people.

The reason they don't generally hang out with the masses is because they don't want to be made wrong for being rich. They worked hard to get there. They feel like the pretty girl who other girls like to criticize because they don't see themselves as pretty. What people can't see themselves having, many times they make wrong. They already get bombarded with requests and pleas for assistance. They don't want to subject themselves to resentment or catch blame for all of the problems in the world. For them, the definition of greed is a willingness to receive more than you're willing to give. If you give a lot, then it stands to reason that you will receive a lot.

They do have compassion for those in need. They would love to teach them how to make money. But understand, these are people who have educated themselves and developed habits and character traits that help them to prosper. Yes, a few of them were just plain ole greedy people but the majority of them were people who are highly principled and exercise a great deal of self-restraint and self-discipline. They want to put their money to good use.

One said, *"I don't give money to poor people because they don't know what to do with it. I don't like to squander my money."*

Another one said, *"Some of the most generous people I've ever met were poor. I admire that so I helped them. We still maintain relationships because their heart is in the right place. Some of the greediest I've ever met were poor too. They wanted more than they were willing to give and they thought that was okay. It's not okay. I wouldn't give them the time of day."*

Both of these men grew up poor. In short, they want to put their money where it will be used wisely. And they want to give to people who will appreciate it and use it wisely, not simply those who need. It's hard for me to fault them for that.

I seemed to get along with everyone in the class, but there was one man who would have absolutely nothing to do with me. He was one of the millionaires. He wouldn't speak or even look at me. I was okay with that. So what. I generally treat people the way they treat people the way they treat me. So on the third day during a ten minute break, I was a little surprised when he walked right up to me and said, *"The five people you hang out with the most will effect your life the most."*

I said, *"Okay, who do you look for?"*

He said, *"Have you taken a class in the last six months? Have you read a book this month? Have you helped someone this week? Have you physically exercised this week? Have you prayed today?"* Then he walked away. He left the class early so we never spoke again.

Before that moment, I didn't know that he was the reason I had come. I didn't know that this was the place I would meet the person who, literally in one minute, would give me a tool I had been looking for my whole entire life. I will be ever thankful.

What he gave me was the recipe for balance. I've made a good bit of money. I've also been homeless twice. I have always been one of those, all in, go for broke, bet the farm people. I would take that double or nothing bet. If there's two minutes on the clock and we're eight points down, give me the ball. A lot of people, I dare say most people play to not lose. I like playing to win. Moderation and I have never been close friends.

Think about this definition:
Wealth is the ability to survive a number of days forward without the addition of more work and without a drop in your lifestyle.

The question then becomes:
How many days forward can you survive if you stop working today? That number of days represents your level of wealth. The objective is to extend that number of days to forever...

Have you taken a class in the last six months?
This builds your intellectual wealth, your intellectual ability to survive a number of days forward...

Have you read a book this month?
A book can affect you directly emotionally, spiritually, or intellectually. In any case a person who can read and does not is as illiterate as a person who cannot read. The smartest people in the world have written things down to preserve their place in posterity. For all practical purposes, the whole expanse of mankind's experience can be found in books. This builds your intellectual, spiritual, or emotional ability to survive a number of days forward...

Have you helped someone this week?
When you help someone, who feels good? You do. This builds your emotional ability to survive a number of days forward...

Have you physically exercised this week?
This builds your physical ability to survive a number of days forward...

Have you prayed today?
This builds you spiritual ability to survive a number of days forward....

What he gave me was a recipe to guide my thoughts to create the habits of building wealth. Wealthy people are not smarter. They just have better habits that generate wealth. I'm not just talking about financial wealth, but wealth in several major areas of your life. I don't have to swan dive off of cliffs to see if I can fly. Good habits don't take away the desire to jump. They give you a parachute. They can't keep you from all harm but they can put a buffer between you and harm. It rains on the good and the bad. Good habits give you an umbrella.

Duty

In the mid 1990's Bill Clinton, then President of the USA, positioned aircraft carriers in the Persian Gulf and started lobbing cruise missiles at Baghdad, Iraq. This was after the first Gulf War. Within a day or two of that time I was at an airport to take a trip. While in the boarding area I sat right across from a clean cut young man. He was about 6'2", skinny, baby face, maybe 18 or 19 years old. He was wearing a full navy uniform, blue bell bottoms, white hat, the works. He had a very serious look on his face.

I asked, *"How long have you been in the service?"*

"Twelve weeks." He said abruptly.

"So you're still in basic training?"

"Just graduated."

I felt like I might have been annoying him a little bit but he was so hard and intense that it seemed kind of amusing.

"That's great. What's your new job?"

"My M.O.S. is..." whatever it was.

"So where are you headed now?"

"I'm assigned to an aircraft carrier in the Persian Gulf."

At that point it wasn't amusing anymore. It suddenly became life and death. Even though he seemed ready to go, he still looked like a kid to me.

I said, *"There's a pretty hot political climate over there. What do you think about that?"*

He stood up at attention, looked me right in my face and said, *"I will do my duty sir!"* He was absolutely clear. He had a job to do. It wasn't about him or how he felt about it at all.

I stood up, gave that young man a full embrace and whispered in his ear, *"I will trust the defense of this nation in your hands. God bless you."* And I meant it. He smiled.

Even now when I have to do something I don't want to do or have to make a hard decision about what is honorable, clean, righteous, or fair, whether it's good for me or not, I think about that young man. Then I say to myself, *"I will do my duty sir."*

Foreclosure

Yeah I missed the January mortgage payment, February too. I was about 20 days late in March when I got the letter. It was a foreclosure notice. It ticked me off. I'm one of the youngest of a bunch of kids growing up so I hate people trying to just take stuff from me – no matter what it is. If they had waited the customary 90 days before filing on me they may have gotten my home without an inordinate amount of resistance. Even I felt like 90 days late is a justifiable filing. But 80 days is a false start. They jumped the gun. It's you trying to bully me and take my stuff. No! Absolutely not! You cannot just strong arm take my house. I'm not going to raise the white flag and let you dismiss me. This is my home. My family has been on this property since the 1920's. It's the land where my fathers' died, land of the Pilgrims pride for me. No! You cannot take my home.

The next day I called them, got to the appropriate department and made this request of the front line person. *"I want you to drop me down to X percent interest rate, stretch me out to 30 years, and I want my payment to be X much."*

Them. *"Let me verify who you are and look up your file. Oh no, no. We can't do that."* She said, then called me by my first name.

I said, *"With all due respect to you, my friends call me by my first name. You're trying to take my money and my home. You address me as Mr. Summers. Let me speak with your manager please."*

(Pause) *"Are you the manager?"*

"Yes."

"Can you make a decision?"

"It depends but generally, yes."

"I want you to drop me down to X percent interest rate, stretch me out to 30 years, and I want my payment to be X much."

Them. *"Oh no, no. We can't do that."*

Me. *"Thank you very much."*

Then I'd call them again the next day with the exact same request for the front line person, then the manager. I did this every day for 8 straight weeks. After that I cut it down to three days a week for another eighteen months straight.

Keep in mind this is a huge mega bank that holds millions of mortgages. I can't even imagine how many thousands of calls they get on a daily basis. After a few weeks they would say, *"Let me verify who you are and look up your file. Your file has been busy."*

After several more weeks they would say, *"Your file is extensive."*

After a few more months they would say, *"Oh, it's you Mr. Summers."*

"Yes it's me. I want you to drop me down to X percent interest, stretch me out to 30 years, ..."

I would tell them things like, *"You don't want my stinky little house in this older depreciating Black neighborhood. It's just a house to you. It's a line item on a spreadsheet. But to me, for all it is or is not, it's still my home. You know crime tends to increase as people lose their jobs. You're still making money on me even at a lower interest rate. If you take my house you're not making any money at all. In fact it will cost you thousands of dollars to foreclose in legal fees, preventing pipes from freezing, cutting grass, getting critters out of the attic, and the general upkeep on a vacant property so you don't lose credibility and collect city fines by looking like a slumlord. I have good neighbors. I'm sure some of my neighbors would be happy to relieve you of all of the appliances, plumbing, wiring, counter tops, cabinets, doors, and whatever else they could help you out with to lessen your burden. They would assume you would want these things in good working condition and put to good use. And you might even have a needy family or two with several children squatting in here. Heck, even I'm going to be looking for a place to live. Don't you agree it would be better for both of us to just drop me down to X percent interest..."*

I would drizzle these considerations out on a weekly basis.

After twenty months a foreclosure representative called me, for a change. She said, *"After reviewing your income and expenses we were wondering if you could find a way to trim about $200 off of your monthly expenses from somewhere? If so, maybe we could make an adjustment on the financing of the property."*

"Why certainly. I don't need $400 a month for food. I could cut that back by 25%. And I could ride my bicycle or take public transportation to work more often so I wouldn't need so much gas in the car. And I'm sure the church and other nonprofits would understand if I cut back on the charitable donations. Yes I think I could do it. Do your numbers work now?"

"Yes Mr. Summers. With those adjustments I believe we could drop your interest rate down several points, stretch you out to 35 years, and reduce your monthly payments to $5 more than what you've been asking for the last 20 months."

In reality, that's not exactly how they said it, but it is what they said. It reduced my payments by several hundred dollars a month and made my life a lot more manageable. And of course they suggested it was their corporate duty to assist good customers in troubling times. I don't want to minimize my gratitude for what they did. I'm very thankful.

The truth is that it was a miracle. I give all due praise to God where it belongs.

Success Guilt

My wife and I lived in a hotel right downtown. In order to have covered parking we had to rent a space a block away. Even in the dead of winter you could handle a one block walk. In the block between home and the car was a discount movie theater where you could catch a $3.00 movie. The place was busy quite often. It was about week before Christmas. After returning from a nice dinner, we parked and headed for home about 9:00 p.m. My wife was wearing a long olive green trench coat, a flat top felt hat with a four inch brim, and matching boots. I had on an extra-long classic London Fog trench coat and a brown high crown Dobbs fedora with a three inch brim. We were not matching but we were coordinated and city clean.

I guess the movie let out at the same time we parked so there were close to a hundred people filing onto the sidewalk. Instead of walking through them we decided to cross the street to avoid the crowd. I checked the crowd while waiting at the light and noticed a man looking at me. I just knew he was up to something so I turned away quickly and crossed. We were the only people on that side of the street. Then here he came shuffling across the four lane street directly toward us. Immediately I pulled out my pocket knife and prepared to perforate this man. I was ready to throw down right now. When he got to the middle of the street, about twenty feet away, I pointed at his face and said, *"STOP RIGHT THERE! What do you want?"* I was angry because he had violated my space when he rushed us like that. That's what robbers do. I was with my wife. I can't let people charge me like that.

"Oh it ain't nothin' man. I just need a dollar so I can get something to eat."

He had shown no respect with a word from far away and a gesture to approach. *"You had money to go the movie. Why didn't you buy something to eat? There's a hundred people over there. Why didn't you ask one of them? Don't try to put the squeeze on me. I'm not your target. Get outta' here."*

He stood there. He was angry too. He said, *"I can see you're rich. I can look at you and see you're rich."*

He had mistaken what I looked like with who I am, and where I'm from. I grew up in a neighborhood with a big stack of people just like him. *"Even if I am rich I don't owe you jack."* I tossed him a quarter and said, *"Get away from me."* He skulked back across the street and blended into the crowd.

We hurried home. This event bothered me for weeks. I felt that I had allowed myself to be used. I had contempt for this man and he had resentment for me. He felt entitled to something for nothing just because he wanted it and thought I had it. He was trying to be slick. It was about exploiting me and he resented when I called him on it. Yet I felt compelled to give him something. It left a bad taste in my mouth. Later I called it '*Success Guilt.*'

Success Guilt is a paradox. I think it happens to people who grew up poor, then later make a substantial amount of money (substantial is certainly a relative term) or someone who acquires a fair bit of influence. When confronted actively or passively with requests from poor people, they may feel compelled to offer money or to pay for things. Giving to be a big shot, which is ego based, is one thing. At least the big shot feels good about it. It is also a noble thing to give out of simple generosity or from the goodness of the heart. I believe helping people in general, including the poor, is a good thing. I have no problem with that.

However, when the giving compulsion comes from tapes running in your head such as:

A) People might think you think you're better than they are.

B) Am I being stingy?

C) Don't act like you just don't care about others.

D) Do others have expectations of me to share with those with less no matter what they did to have less?

E) Am I being greedy?

F) Is this how rich people act?

The list could be extensive. I had to examine myself. Is it right for some random person, or even people I know, to have an expectation of me to share with them no matter what? There is no harm in asking but I don't owe you. Is this how rich people think/act, etc.? I didn't put them in that situation. Would you rather make yourself poorer than subject yourself to those tapes? It felt like an act of submission. Another indicator is that you don't feel good about it. That quarter represented a whole lot more than 25 cents.

Finally a few months later, I pulled a wealthy acquaintance to the side and told him about this situation and how I felt about it. He asked me, *"Do you work hard for your money?"*

"Yes."

"Then why do you feel obligated to give it to someone you don't even like? It's okay to say no to people. You don't have to get upset about it. Those with means really should help those in need. Wealthy people give away tremendous amounts of money. One of the blessings of having money is you can make choices. You can share it. That's honorable. There's nothing wrong with that. But make sure it's something you can feel good about."

I really don't mind helping out. I hope that every life I touch is better just because they met me, even if it's just a smile or opening a door. If the man had approached me respectfully I might have gladly helped him out too. I know what it is to be in need.

There have been times when I've helped out too much or too often. After a while I felt like they thought of me like their personal banker. It really didn't help them. It just made them more dependent. Then they felt entitled. And in the end, they resented me. It was as if I did them wrong if I didn't give or lend them money. There is no joy anywhere for me the giver or them the receiver. In this case it was a predatory stranger but it could just as easily have been a member of my own family.

When your world gets bigger you have to grow. You can't go back to who you were. It can be painful because sometimes you outgrow people you love, even friends or some members of your family. You can't help by throwing money at the issue. I want to uplift people. I want to help others solve problems. But I can't help by making other people's problems my problems. If you recognize the problem and you want to help solve it then sow a seed. Create opportunities, systems, structures, and artifacts. Be generous. Educate people. Or walk away. It may not be your battle. If you care, you have to give of yourself or it has no meaning. When you do that, everybody wins. There's no guilt.

Precession

Generalized principles are principles that are true in all cases. There are several of them. They affect all of us all of the time physically, spiritually, emotionally, intellectually, financially, and other ways I may have no concept of. They always work. Precession is a generalized principle.

Precession as I understand it ***is the law of bodies in motion on other bodies in motion.*** The components of precession are attraction = magnetism, velocity = speed, and mass = density. It always occurs at a 90 degree angle. It's physics. A procession is to go in a straight line like a parade. Precession radiates outwardly, omni-directionally (in every direction).

Here is an example. A honey-bee will fly to a flower on a horizontal axis. Her goal is to get the nectar. That's all she cares about. When she gets the nectar, she's a happy girl. In the process, she will stick her nose into the flower and shake her furry little body. Consequently and seemingly inadvertently, by coincidence, by happenstance, on a vertical axis (at a 90 degree angle to the direction of her flight) pollen will fall onto her fury little body. She cares nothing about this. The pollen is totally, coincidental, inconsequential, and superfluous to her. It is a moot point to her. She will then fly on a horizontal axis to a second flower and do the same thing. Consequently, on a vertical axis, more pollen will fall onto her furry little body. But in the process also on a vertical axis, some pollen will fall off thus pollinating the second flower.

Realize that the honey-bee may do this hundreds of times a day on a horizontal axis. Her only goal is to get the nectar. That's all she cares about. When she gets the nectar, she's a happy girl. But God's goal on a vertical (90 degree) axis is to pollinate the fields.

So I ask myself as a honey money bee, what nectar can I want? What goal can I choose on a horizontal axis that God's goal of better energy use, housing, health care, food production, entertainment, and/or education can fall out on a vertical axis.

These are things that fundamentally and directly help to improve life on the planet for mankind (Buckminster Fuller).

Here is another example. You have a pebble and you drop it into a pond of water. The pebble will fall on a vertical axis but when it hits the water at a 90-degree angle to the horizontal plane of the water, it will create a ripple. But the ripple doesn't just go in one direction. It goes in every direction (omni-directionally). That is the precessional effect of the pebble falling into the water.

In the same way, everything we do or don't do has a precessional effect. You are creating a ripple all of the time. The question is, what kind of ripple are you creating and what would you actually like to create?

(I got all of this from a Buckminster Fuller concept.)

******

On a cold winter day in downtown Milwaukee, two of my team and I were in the mall. We had a shop there and we were doing our retail thing with our black slacks, white shirts, vests, and ties on, as usual. Shortly after opening, I noticed a young man watching me from about thirty feet away. He was about 6'2", handsome and street clean. He wore a long black leather trench, $200 sneakers, jewelry around his neck and on every finger. He watched me for close to half an hour before he finally approached.

He said, *"You're from the hood, right?"*

"Yeah.."

"Can we talk?"

"Yeah."

"Between me and you?"

"Yeah man. What I know, I know. It's me and you. We're there"

He said, *"My name is John. I'm in the self-medication pharmaceutical business. I'm in the drug business. I have four people working for me and I make bank. But every day my conscious bothers me. I was not raised up like this. I'm ashamed of what I do. I got a wife and two kids. I can't let them down. I can't help them in jail. Can you teach me how to be a real business man like you?"*

I put my arm around his shoulder and said, *"Son, you're already a real business man. You just have a lousy product. It kills people. Every time you buy another big package, they call that 'an expenditure of capital for wholesale commodity acquisition.' When you break it down into smaller pieces, it's called 'packaging for retail distribution.' That's real business. Now let's see how we can make it right."*

We went up to the food court and I explained precession just like I did above. I talked about the honeybee and about dropping pebbles in a pond. He got it completely. Then I asked him, *"What happens if you sell just one hit of crack just one time?"*

"Not much. Somebody gets high. No big deal."

"Okay, what happens if you sell one hit of crack all day every day?"

"That's what I'm doing now. I make bank."

"Yeah, but what happens to those who are buying the crack? And what do you attract?" We went through this process for about an hour. As he came up with answers, all I would say is, *"And what else?"*

Ultimately, the answers he came up with were: *The loss of respect of respectable people, loss of income, loss of jobs, loss of a tax base, unsafe community, breakup of families, violence, imprisonment, death.*

Then I asked him, *"If you simply changed your product to blue jeans and do everything else the same as you're doing it right now, what happens?"*

What he came up with was: *The gaining of respect from respectable people, the increase of the tax base, people get hired, a more stable community, families come together. They write articles in the newspaper about what a great business he runs.* We got up. He left. I went back to work. I didn't see him anymore after that.

*****

A year and a half passed. It was a beautiful summer day about mid-morning and I was riding down a semi-busy street when I passed a cleared out vacant lot. There was a straight panel truck parked in the lot with the doors flung wide open. I barely glanced at it as I passed by. The windows were down and I heard someone whistle for me from the lot. Ninety nine percent of the time I would just keep rolling but this time the little voice in my head said to go back and check it out. So I did.

As I pulled slowly into the lot, I actually looked at the lot, the surroundings, inside, under, and behind the truck to make sure it wasn't some kind of set up. I had my getaway mapped out.

Hanging on the inside of both doors on multiple hooks were NBA and pro football jerseys, starter team jackets, sneakers, and sweat suits in several sizes and colors. From the ground leading up to the back of the truck were stairs so that anyone could come in and see what else might be available. At the top of the stairs stood the young man I had talked to well over a year ago. With arms spread wide and even a bigger smile, he looked at me and said, *"PRECESSION!"*

Mastery

A master is an ordinary person who gets extraordinary results consistently. I can think of four different levels of mastery.

The *lowest level of mastery* is the Midas touch. For those who have it, everything they touch turns to gold. They're gifted. Other people simply can't do what they seem to do with ease. They have laser focus and a high degree of skill in their field of expertise. Michael Jordan, Donald Trump, Julia Roberts, Warren Buffet, Harrison Ford, and Oprah Winfrey have it. Michael Jackson had it for decades (although later he got sidetracked). My grandmother had it in the kitchen. She could boil rocks and it would taste like a banquet. People want to be around them just to see what they're doing. They make things look easy that you know are difficult. Everybody has good days. Sometimes it's just your day. They get into the zone regularly.

Caution:

1) There are a few things they should look out for. Sometimes they are so overpowering and take up so much space that they may not see or leave room for others to shine. They are not always great team players.

2) Sometimes they can be obsessive. That's okay as long as they are doing what they're great at. But they can get themselves into trouble when they obsess about diversionary things such as changing their field of focus, gambling, collecting multiple women, etc.

These are people who can put a team or a project on their back and carry the day. They can do a tremendous amount of whatever it is on their own. They are sole proprietors, even innovators who are the best one around at what they do. They create. They are superstars. They can take care of themselves.

The *next higher level of mastery* are those who, when they are around other people, get better. Their stats may or may not be impressive independently but the stats of everyone around them get better. They find what people are strong at. They are students of their craft. They are both intuitive and analytical. They put pieces together. They don't normally think of themselves as stars. They think everyone else is a star and then set out to prove it. They have a big field of vision. They find or put people in the right place. They seem to make themselves indispensable. They pass the ball or give the part to the star. They anticipate other peoples' needs and make them look good. They don't need a lot. Most of the time they can work wonders with very little and get far more done than it appears. They normally don't ever get the credit they deserve. They're easy not to notice. You may not recognize them as the facilitator or conductor. But they are sorely missed when they're not around. With them, everybody wins. Magic Johnson and Larry Bird have it. Kevin Spacey, Jeena Davis, and Joan Kusak have it. Multi-tasking wives, secretaries, administrative assistants, good nurses, and teachers have it. They are a catalyst for others to be better. They do what is needed. They take pride in service. They are outstanding support people. They take care of themselves and help other people to be the best they can be.

The *next higher level of mastery* is those who can take lumps of coal and bring out the diamond in them. They can see the diamond before it is visible. Michael Angelo said something like, "*A beautiful sculpture is already inside a block of marble. All I do is chip away at what covers it up.*" That's what these masters do. They are motivators, and challengers of people to be better than they are now. They are small business owners, school principals, coaches, and mentors. The most important and common examples of them are parents. These are people who expect more of you than you do of yourself. When you fall they feel the pain. They take you to the edge of your comfort zone safely and then ask more of you. You would do things for them that you don't want to do or would never do for yourself. They see the greatness in you despite your flaws and push you towards excellence. They bring out the greatness in other people. These are not formula people. They go where you are. They will customize their own lives to make your life work. These are the people who tick us off. They push our buttons. At the time, we wish they would leave us alone even though we know what they want from us will help us. We tend to cherish them later. For the rest of our lives we hear their voices in our heads and hope that we can somehow come close to what they saw in us. They believe in us. They see the greatness in others, can draw it out, and teach that person to sustain it. They develop people who can take care of other people.

Those with the *highest level of mastery* are those who can teach masters to teach masters to teach masters... How do you know if you're a good parent? What are your children doing when you're not around? How do you know if you're a great parent? What are your grandchildren and great grandchildren doing? Did you teach someone to teach someone? With these masters you see generational growth. You may or may not recognize how well they do what they do at the time they're doing it. Only later and usually decades, centuries, or even millennium later can we see the impact of what they've done. It's not unusual for them to be ridiculed or persecuted in their own time. These are the visionaries who create a way of thinking, a way of being. They have a philosophy and then create a system to fit the philosophy. They have followers who study them. Spin offs, innovations, and interpretations come from their work. Things or movements get named after them.

They break things down to their lowest common denominator and reconfigure the parts. They invent new parts or new uses for parts. To them, genius is born in simplicity. What they do makes so much sense that it is ridiculous to go back to the previous norm. Their peers will scratch their heads and wonder '*Why didn't I think of that?*' Some examples would be, Jesus Christ, and Mohammad in religion; Newton, and Einstein in physics; Shakespeare, Thomas Edison, and Alexander Graham Bell in lighting and sound; Henry Ford in mass production; John Wooden in basketball, Mary Kay in marketing, Steve Jobs in personal electronics, Chuck Barry, James Brown and The Beatles in modern music. In all cases, their philosophies and impact endure over continents, cultures, and time. They create ways of thinking or doing things that endure long after they're gone. They take care of masses.

*****

One of the keys to mastery is to surround yourself with people who expect more of you than you do of yourself. Find people who challenge you to be greater than you currently demonstrate. They help you to see a bigger picture from which a true purpose can develop. Once you have a purpose you have a direction. It gives you clarity. You may not know where it will take you but you do know when you're not headed that way. Clarity leads to power. Clarity leads to manifestation.

Clarity helps you to make finer distinctions. Making finer distinctions is another key to mastery. Think about it. The difference between success and failure, between first and second can easily be less than one percent, from 49 to 51 percent or less. The difference between mediocrity and excellence may be five percent. It's the consistent extra effort that gives you the opportunity to find the detail. It puts you on the trail to where mastery lives. When you do your absolute best, when you strive for excellence, it automatically bumps you up to the top 10 percent in whatever you do. People can forgive what you don't know. They will not forgive your lack of effort or your lack of sincerity. When you match your best efforts with something you have a talent for and a keen eye, with good fortune you can then enter the realm of mastery.

Masters are always striving to improve. Many are willing but not able. Others are able but not willing. These masters are both. Whatever they do, no matter how fantastic, they feel like it wasn't quite enough. Maybe they could have done more. They tinker and tweak all the time. They come early and leave late. They practice in the rain. They do the work. The world is littered with talented geniuses. It is the purpose, commitment, clarity, and effort that propel the few to mastery.

Book Three

Relationships

Relationships are built on trust or the lack of trust.

Clues to know where you are in relationship.

thing or a need for validation. That's not for me to say. I don't know what people are thinking or how they feel. I just know what they do. They don't necessarily mean you any harm. It's not about you. It's about them.

Many times their ploys work. They get what they want. The problem is the other person sometimes doesn't feel good about the interaction. They may feel used, manipulated, played, or diminished and will avoid you if possible. It can deplete someone's good will for you. Although when two sharks go at it, they can do it for hours, days, even years locked in a ploy fest. Getting to advantage on the other is the basis of their relationship and they use different ploys to do it. They might even like each other. Go figure.

A ploy once recognized is no longer a ploy.

Rule # 4. Provocability...

When pushed with the force of ten, push back with the force of eight. Why? I push back with the force of eight because if I push back with the force of ten the situation could escalate. I don't want to escalate the issue. I don't care if they feel like they got the better of me. But I also want them to know that if you bite me on purpose, I bite back. I'm number five of six boys growing up. I know that even if they have the advantage, bullies don't like getting hit back.

*****

I couldn't find my daughter for ten years. One Friday morning about 2:00 I was flipping through the channels and saw a ten second ad saying, *"We find people."* I wrote the number down. That night out of the blue, her mother called me and gave me her phone number. She was 19 years old by then.

I called right away and sent for her the next week. It was around Christmas time. On the first night she, my mother, my wife, and I were watching a movie. I said something to my wife. I don't

64

remember what it was. My daughter said to me, *"I don't like the way you talk to your wife."*

I asked her to come to another room with me. The radio happened to be playing. I told her, *"You can't tell me how to talk to my wife. If it's not an issue for her, and I'm not harming or abusing her, you have no right to interfere. This is my wife."*

She said, *"If you do it again, I can go home."*

I said, *"I love you. I'm very happy to see you. I don't want you to go. But yes you can go home. I bought you a round trip ticket and if you think you can tell me how to talk to my wife in my own home then you can use it. I'll keep working towards you anyway. God willing, I figure we have another 30 years to work it out."*

I could see tears welling up in her eyes. This is me pushing back with the force of eight. The stakes were very high yet these are principles I try to live by.

I know God was smiling on us that very moment. A song I love came on the radio. It was the perfect dance record. I said, *"Hold on sweetheart. We can argue later. We can't waste this jam."* I took her by the hand and spun her around. We danced and smiled like a dad dancing with his little girl. By the time the song was over the tension was dissipated. We both still love that song. It was the grace of God.

*****

Rule # 5. Willingness to walk away…

Sometimes the relationship is just too hard, too painful, too toxic, or maybe it just doesn't matter enough to salvage. Then it's time to walk away.

Drama/Trust Scale

It is my belief that relationships are built on trust or the lack of trust. This is one way I assess where I am in a relationship.

When the drama is high and the trust is low, I'm shark bait. I'm the tuna.

High drama + Low trust = I'm shark bait

When the drama is high and the trust is high, you can have a breakthrough.

High drama + High trust = Breakthrough

When the drama is low and the trust is low there is basically no relationship.

Low drama + Low trust = No relationship

When the drama is low and the trust is high you have a great relationship.

Low drama + High trust = Great relationship

High Drama/Low Trust

I have older brothers. My oldest brother is almost 16 years older than I am. I've always called him the golden boy. He was the first and only of 11 grandchildren for six or seven years with adoring grandparents and several aunts and uncles. The rest of us stair stepped after that. There must be a million pictures of him around the house. By the time I got here, I guess they felt like, "*We know what you look like.*" So I have the obligatory school class pictures. He was smart, good looking, tall and athletic. He was an honor roll student all the way through high school. He was also an all-state running back in football. Then he went on to a big ten university when there were only a few Black students in all of those schools combined. He played on the Rose Bowl team in 1964 and won. This was right at the height of the big civil rights marches and demonstrations, the '*I Have a Dream*' speech, etc. He really was a handsome, smart, athletic, big ten graduate, ready to go to work just in time to be the highly sought after Black college grad to showcase in your corporate brochure. No slur on him, he, in fact, was qualified for the jobs. He was six feet three and would run 1000 steps on each foot, do 100 sit ups and 100 pushups every day well into his fifties. He later owned a business and then became a minister. Was he the golden boy or what?

He was a great guy. The problem for all of the rest of us 'little ones' was that we couldn't tell him anything. He already knew everything. He had a high need to be right with us, his younger siblings, even though all of the rest of us were smart too. We all have strong likes, dislikes, and opinions just like he does. One difference was the rest of us always had to work together and share everything. He never had to share. Maybe it's just a big brother thing but I tend to think that in his mind, he had a greater identity association with our elders in the previous generation than with us, the little ones. He was the only child among a lot of adults for a long time. Even though he was our older brother, it's like he thought of himself as 'Mr. Older Brother' with all entitled due deference in line with his position. This may be a slight exaggeration but if you would, imagine being the younger sibling of a king who feels like God made him the king. How do you get around that?

In all fairness to him, in the world at large, he was reasonable, rational, charming, and giving. He would regularly go above and beyond the call of duty to help people and our community as a whole. He was a true leader over all. That being said, at home, he was respected and loved even if he was a bit pompous and self-important.

All of this prelude is to say he understood competition very well. If you disagreed with him sometimes he took it as a challenge instead of an opportunity to see another point of view. So when the drama got high at home, the trust was low. I was shark bait. He didn't necessarily understand cooperation. He understood competition. He didn't necessarily want to solve the problem. He wanted to win. He wanted to be right. Not only that, but he felt we should be loyal and agreeable to him and his point of view, whatever that may be.

He would even say, *"I'm the eldest and major decisions ought to be deferred to me."* And as he pointed his finger in the air would proclaim, *"And by law, blah, blah blah."*

He had no conflict with this. Where do you go from there? Thus, you see the problem. So when issues got hot, he wanted to win. He was willing to go for the jugular or take his ball, go home, and leave you swinging in the wind.

So, when issues got hot and the drama was high, the trust was low. I would have to go for his jugular (Something I didn't want to do. For all he is or isn't, he's still my brother.) or get out of the game quickly.

In the end, he left us in the year 2000. And to his great credit, he ultimately found humility.

High Drama/High Trust

My second brother, who I call my big brother, is an easy-going guy. I call him my big brother because even though he was a kid himself, he is the one who would make sure us younger ones were fed and our needs were met. He would explain how and why things work, not just try to boss us around. He would put me on the handlebars and take me with him on his paper route and other places with his friends. He was, without question, the best of the bunch academically when he wanted to be. Getting him to want to be is a different matter. He was extremely strong willed but not driven like my older brother. He wanted to do what he wanted to do. He wasn't a bad kid. He was a daring, push-the-envelope kid. I think he was a gifted child before they knew what to do with Black academically gifted children. He was a state champion gifted athlete as well. He would get bored though. Then there was no telling what he might do. He's the one who showed me a Playboy magazine when I was about eight years old. I thought it was gross. *"Eewww! You're so nasty! What do you like that for?"* He could not stop laughing. I can still see him cracking up and trying to catch his breath about that.

So when the drama gets high, the trust is also high. One of us will concede or we'll find another way. He understands cooperation. I know he would never purposely harm me. We can have a breakthrough.

Low Drama/Low Trust

When the drama is low and the trust is low, there is basically no relationship. You may have this relationship with people who you know but don't really have a lot to do with like co-workers, people you are in an organization with, and even some relatives. These are the people you have no great affinity or ill will for. You might like them but if you don't see them for a while, it doesn't bother you a bit.

Low Drama/High Trust

When the drama is low and the trust is high, this is a great relationship. This is what you want in all of your close relationships. Good luck with that. Bankers love this kind of relationship. You have been on the job for five years or more, you own a home and a car with no 30- day late payments, and have a 700+ credit score. You don't even have to call them. They'll call you to give you a loan or a credit card.

We all know people who go from crisis to crises or who always have some kind of drama going on in their lives. I tend to keep an emotional distance from them. I don't want to get sucked in. I don't want their problems to become my problems. I think they have a hard time getting to joy or happy so they create drama. It makes them feel alive. I've had to end meaningful relationships just to get off the rollercoaster. If I can't get to happy I at least want peace. I have bells that go off loudly the instant drama rises even a little bit. If I want drama in my life, I'll go to a party, take a class, or get a hobby. Otherwise, I want a low drama high trust life.

Deaf Culture Experience

Snow plows had piled mounds of snow high enough to hide a car behind. It was a Friday evening, February 4th, 2011. The temperature was in the single digits as I pulled into the parking lot of a big strip mall in northern Illinois where a book store was located. It was 7:15 p.m. There was nothing on the events board just inside the door so I asked both clerks at the desk to point me to the gathering of deaf people in the store. Neither one knew anything about it. That's when I walked over to the coffee counter and I saw them.

There were five women signing away and laughing just like any other group of friends having a conversation. I stood about fifteen feet away at another table and wrote this note, *"My name is Summers. I am taking a basic sign language class. I hardly know anything but I heard about your group and wanted to come. Is that okay with you? I already know that you sign faster than I can see."*

They checked me out as I approached and put the note on the table. They passed it around, signed something, laughed, and welcomed me warmly. I imagined they signed something about my good looks. This was there fourth meeting.

Only one of them was deaf. One had just graduated from a community college translator course. The others were still taking classes. By 8:00 p.m there were fifteen people.

They naturally formed a big oval so everyone could see each other. There were no secrets in there as far as I could tell. I introduced myself a lot. *"My name is Summers. Your name is what? Good to meet you?"*

Now there were six men, and nine women. Three of the women had been deaf their whole lives. One could speak and came with a speaking friend. One came with her mother and brother both of whom could speak but signed very well. She could sign at a mile a minute. Only the most experienced signers could keep up with her. I heard that most families are not quite that supportive. They seemed very close. The third lady was a well-respected translator/instructor. The man was an instructor at the Center for Deafness in Northbrook, Illinois. He had lost his hearing later. There's a sign for that. He was a laid back signer and easy to understand. Everyone else could speak but would only do so to teach or to clarify. I'm pretty sure that most of those who could speak initially learned to sign to be able to communicate with someone they cared about. Most people mouthed and signed at the same time. A few people were excellent lip readers as well. From what I gathered, you can be a dominant left or right handed signer as long as you are consistent. Other signers will understand. I mostly spoke and lettered. You can pick up a lot by paying attention although the two ladies at my side graciously translated for me. I realized how important context is. The ladies informed me about the different levels of licenses, certificates, kinds of work, and other forums to engage with deaf culture.

Two Latino guys came in a little after 9:00 p.m. One was animated, larger than life. Several people got up to hug him. That's apparently a big deal. He was a tutor to many, and much more. He's a naval officer/translator with three translators under him. He signs in four languages. Even though I didn't understand most of what he was saying, I could tell he was funny. He asked my name. I lettered it to him. He confirmed and then, out of nowhere he just gave me a name. *"Your name is Summer."* Our instructor said it could happen and it did.

As I arose to leave, I thanked them in sign. They asked me to come again. It was a good experience. It felt like being in a different country where another language is spoken then realizing that everywhere, people are just people. I noticed a smile on my face as I left the building.

The Back Story

As a young man of 20 or 21, I had a good friend who played in a local baseball league so I went to see him play. It was a warm evening in the summer time. I was sitting in the bleachers when I looked over and saw a pretty young lady sitting by herself. I went over to speak, and offered her a piece of candy. She smiled, received it and said, *"Thank you."* That's when I noticed her voice sounded like people who can't hear well. She was deaf but I didn't care about that. We sat together, talked and laughed. She was animated and fun to be with. We were cracking up. We figured out the communication thing. She made it easy for me. She could read lips and gestured better than anyone I've ever seen. I liked her a lot. We started going out.

My friends would ask me, *"Why her?"*

I'd say, *"Because I like her and she likes me. She's smart, sweet, pretty, and cooler than any of your girlfriends ever will be."*

They would flip me the finger and we'd laugh.

We even went dancing one time. She could feel the music in her body and that girl could really shake it up. She would teach me basic signs. We went places and did summertime things that couples do. She was great.

One day we were hanging out and I did something that made her angry. She started to fuss at me in that voice. I thought it was funny and started to laugh. Maybe it had happened to her before with other people; maybe too many times. It was a stupid, insensitive thing to do. I hurt that girl. I hurt her feelings. I didn't mean to but I did. I realized too late that my behavior was offensive and disrespectful. She wouldn't see me anymore after that and never spoke to me again.

She probably has grown children by now, maybe grandchildren. But every time I hear that voice or see someone signing I think of her. I've always wanted to tell her how sorry I was. So in 2011, decades later, I took an American Sign Language 101 class. It was my way of telling her how much I really cared.

Kiss Him Too

"Finally grown up" could have been written on their T shirt. It's amazing what you can deduce or maybe just imagine at a glance when put in context. They looked so young and content meandering around this beautiful garden center looking at shrubs and smelling the flowers. You had to feel good for them.

It was probably their first home. They looked like one of those couples who had been raised in the suburbs and moved to the city after college. You know the story. Get the great job. Meet someone. Get married. Get the cool city condo in the right neighborhood. When she gets pregnant, they find a nice starter home in the suburbs with the parents help on the down payment.

They were pushing a Cadillac stroller too. I asked the mother, *"Is this your first?"* I knew it was because the first baby always gets the doting parents, the Cadillac stroller, a thousand pictures, and the brand new best of everything. The rest of the kids get the backyard, school pictures, and the 'value purchased' everything although all of the children are equally loved.

"Would you like a key to a happy home?"

"Yes tell me."

"I have grown children with children so I'm talking to you like I talk to them. This is grandfather talk.

We love our children. They look like us. And they act like us. That's a double edged sword because they can out do you doing you. But be mindful, these little darlings might grow up and leave you for someone you don't even like. They will be embarrassed when you drop them off in front of the school when they're twelve years old and break your heart. "Give me a ride. Give me some money. Drop me off a block away. And don't kiss me."

So here's the key:

Every time you kiss your children, kiss your husband too. Fathers love their children. You want him to love you. If you and he are okay, the kids will be okay. And later, when the kids don't have time for you, you want him at his second job thinking about his desert when he gets home.

Understand, children are so attractive they can consume you. We're programmed that way. For a good while all kids think about is, "Please me. Do for me. Make me happy." And we want to do it. The problem is if you put your husband second behind your children, ultimately he may put you second behind his job, a hobby, a sports team, etc. When the children grow up they will put you second as well. They have to build a life for themselves. Then you may be puzzled or disheartened when you and your husband have grown apart. He doesn't pay much attention to you, doesn't include you, doesn't want to do things with you, or worse, pays too much attention to something else or someone else.

It may not be fair, but we men expect women to bring the sweetness and joy to our homes. We may not receive it but it's what we always hope for. Just like you may not receive it but you hope for us to work and provide for the family.

Greet him at the door with a smile on your face. Rub up against him a little bit. You know how to do it. We like that. Get his attention. It's a way to connect. We don't mind facing the storm of life. We don't want to come home to the storm of life. This could easily be the best moment of his day. This could the reason he's willing to face it again tomorrow. Then give him thirty minutes before you get on his case. Let him take a breath. I know it's a lot to ask for you to be sweet like that all the time, especially considering the busy day you've had. Plus I know you've seen us screw things up and maybe even blame you for it. You've seen us in awkward situations or with bad colds looking horrible. You've seen us fart, snore, and slobber in the bed. But greet us warmly anyway.

75

Some women are natural mothers. Some are natural wives. If you are a natural wife, you don't need this conversation but you may need to nurture your children a little more. If not, work on it to keep your relationship with him more close. It can pay off in the long run. That's a key to a happy home."

What Is Team – What Is Trust?

In the early 90's I took a class called 'Business School for Entrepreneurs.' There were about 150 people in the class held at a beautiful resort in Hawaii. There were only six Americans. Everyone else was from Australia, New Zealand, Singapore, Canada, Germany, South America, etc. It was a seventeen day class.

On the first day an instructor asked everyone to come to the front and put $250 (American) in a big box that was sitting on a table. Everyone did that. Then she asked us to count off individually from one to twelve. Those with the same number were on a team together. She told us the reason why we have teams is because on day 15 or 16 we would run a race. The race only had two rules. First, your team must finish together or you are disqualified. Second, winner takes all. There was over $35,000 in that box. Everyone then met with his or her respective teams for about 30 minutes.

I had no idea that this race was going to change my life. I was in my mid-thirties, a business owner, and did not know nor care about the race. All I cared about was the data like finance, accounting, production, marketing, sales, and distribution. This was supposed to be Business School for Entrepreneurs run by global oriented business people and my intent was to learn what they know. The race and the other students were really just part of the backdrop to me. I didn't come to run a race or to make friends. My purpose for coming was clear. What I actually got was vastly different.

I stood back about fifteen feet from my newly acquired teammates and watched them. There were eleven White guys from Australia and New Zealand and one White woman from Canada. She was drop dead gorgeous. I mean "stop the car, this babe is fine" kind of gorgeous. She was a personal trainer named Anna and these guys swarmed her. *"I'm the man." "No, no, I'm the man."* is what they appeared to be saying from a distance.

I thought, '*What a sorry group of men to frantically rush her like a bunch of attention starved puppies. Where is your pride?*' I wanted to intercede for her but that was her cross to bear, not mine.

I was a big guy weighing 297 pounds. I was one Happy Meal away from 300. One guy walked over to me and asked if I was on their team.

"Yes" I replied.

Then he looked me up and down like an inspector and said, *"You're not going to hold us up are you?"* At that point I was totally fed up with this team already. I spewed some obscenities at him and told him to get out of my face. Then I went to go meet the rest of them.

"I'm so and so and I'm from this place or that, and blah, blah, blah." is how each person introduced him or herself.

I said, *"My name is Jerome Summers and it won't be me who holds up this team. That's all I have to say."*

Outside, there was a mountain that rose about a mile up at a 45% angle, another two and a half miles across the top, and three fourths of a mile down back to the clubhouse. There was also a bay out there about two football fields wide at its farthest point. We figured that both would be a part of the race.

When we re-convened, out of 150 people, the instructor called me out to ask what I thought about my team. I said, *"Frankly, I don't like them at all. They're just a bunch of foreigners to me."* And I heard a collective grown from the class. Americans were the foreigners to all but six of us. I didn't care. I came to get the data.

Class began a 7:00 a.m. sharp and ended at 11:00 p.m. So the running team met at 5:00 a.m. There was also a marketing team that met after 11:00 p.m. so basically that meant sleep next month. The schedule would be brutal.

The next morning we met at 5:00 a.m. and began our quest to run this mountain and win the prize. It was already 80 degrees. Up we go. I feel like I'm dying but I'm not quitting. It won't be me who holds up this team. That was imperative to me. I would tell myself, '*If I can just make it to that tree, that fire hydrant, that parked car, etc.*' Day one, day two, I made it slowly but made it none the less. Day three, I got to the top but while going across, I started to hyperventilate. I felt like I was going to throw up. My eyes flipped back, and my knees turned into rubber. One person took my right arm, another took my left. A third put his hand in the small of my back. The team leader, Anna, started calling cadence right in front of me while running backwards. And for another two miles my feet went one-two-three-four, one-two-three-four. By the time we got back to the clubhouse, I understood the power of a team.

Team is: *two or more combined for a common purpose working in a spirit of harmony.*

If there is no common purpose it's not team.

If there is no harmony it's not team.

With no common purpose or no harmony, it's just an assortment of people doing things together. I'm the youngest in my immediate family of six. I think they were just an odd assortment of people living together until I got there. I'm sure they would dispute this.

We hear people say a chain is as strong as its' weakest link. That's not team. Team is more like the spokes on a bicycle wheel. When one spoke gives out, the others still support and the wheel keeps rolling. That's team. Team adds mass. To like each other is nice but not necessary. But a common purpose and a spirit of harmony is essential.

How do you know who's on your team?

Who shows up when needed? Where are their feet?

How do you know whose team you're on?

Where do you show up when needed? Where are your feet? How do you spend your time and your money?

On the fourth day we figured we had better start practicing the swim. The problem was, there was only one other man and myself who didn't know how to swim. I wasn't scared of the water. I just couldn't swim. Four people stepped up to teach, two for each of us. My two swim coach team members and I got started. One was from Australia, the other from New Zealand. I remember thinking, *'These guys live on islands. They've probably been swimming since before they could walk.'* I walked into the water up to my neck.

The waves seemed huge. I grew up on Lake Michigan where the waves only get this large during a storm. But there we were in the Pacific Ocean on a calm morning and these waves were rolling. Another challenge for me was, here are these two White guys with their little heads bobbing up and down in the water saying to me, *"Here's what you do and here's what we'll do. If you get in trouble, no worries mate, she'll be right."*

Let me give you some background. I am from a Black community where one of the first things you learn is, *'Don't trust White people especially with your life.'* Nobody has to talk about it. It's a given. It's common knowledge. X = don't trust White people. Everybody knows that.

So here are these two guys saying, *"No worries mate, she'll be right."*

And from my venomous core came these words, *"NO! I don't trust you."*

They looked at me with confusion and cocked their heads sideways like the RCA dog. I turned around and faced the black sand beach. At that point, this thought popped up, '*Summers, you can take your feet off of the bottom and stroke or you can be a little punk standing by the shore for the rest of your life. What are you going to do?*' Immediately, I took my feet off of the bottom and stroked.

In that instant, I had two huge epiphanies. One was about my own racism. All White people are not your enemy and all Black people are not your brother. The other was about trust. It is my belief that relationships are built on trust or the lack of trust.

*****

Trust is: *the ability to put your wellbeing into someone or something else's hands.*

--It involves confidence plus risk.

--If there is no confidence, there is no trust.

--If there's no risk, there's no trust or maybe no need to trust. (I have put some thought into this and it can be challenged. Example... A lot of people say they believe in God. But they don't actually trust God. Although to those who have faith, there is no perceptible risk in trusting God. I have a brother I totally trust and know would never purposely harm me. I would jump in a fox hole with him. I would trust him with my life, my wife, and my money.

--Just because you don't trust doesn't mean the other person is not trustworthy.

--You can't get there from here. You have to go there to be there. In other words you have to take your feet off of the bottom and stroke in order to know if you can trust.

--How do you build trust? You make small agreements and you keep them.

--How do you gauge trust? Listen to what people say and then look at what they do.

--If it is a big agreement get it in writing.

All of this came to me the instant I took my feet off of the bottom and stroked.

There were many more fine distinctions and lessons I learned from the preparation for the race, as well as the race itself. I got these lessons in my body at a cellular level. What I learned in the race was actually the data I came for. And those lessons propelled my business. Over a decade later, I still stay in touch with some of my classmates. Some have been to my home and stayed with my family. I have been to their homes abroad and stayed with their families. I went to that class as an African American but I left as a global citizen. This "*bunch of foreigners to me*" have become a bunch of friends to me.

Secure the Perimeter

Job # 1. The number one job of the leader of any nation, company, organization, street gang, or any head of household is to secure the perimeter and keep harm away from your people. Furthermore, there are several perimeters to be secured: physical, spiritual, emotional, financial, intellectual, and possibly more.

You must secure the outside and from within. Outside you have thieves, liars, hackers, busy bodies, scammers, scalawags, intruders, and barbarians at the gate poking around all the time looking for a weakness. That's what they do. You must secure from within. Those who would commit treason, sabotage, and collusion come from the inside.

To secure the perimeter is a defensive measure. It is to guard against loss or harm. However, as virtuous as it may be, it is not expansive by nature. It does not generally inspire. If taken to the extreme, it can produce paranoia; cause one to become insular, narrow thinking, self-important, etc. It is important to remember that most people are good people and the vast majority of them live outside your perimeter. Also most opportunities to be expansive are out there too. Inside the perimeter can be a world unto itself. It can be a very small place. Think of it as a nest to defend even though you have wings to fly and a whole world you can explore. Think of it as developing an insurance plan.

Treason comes from the inside.

Treason – It can get you or someone else killed.

      - It is a betrayal of trust.

       - It is giving aid and comfort to the enemy.

       - Action must be taken right away.

- It is punishable by death or banishment.

Examples:

-Double agents

-Selling government or trade secrets to another country

-Adultery

Barbarians are at the gate trying to get in all the time. Treason is giving, selling, or trading military or government secrets, plans, equipment, etc. to other countries, or organizations who would or could harm you with it. Corporate espionage and leaks are treason as well.

On a personal level, adultery is a form of treason. Also for a parent or other family members to allow anyone to come into their home and mistreat them, or other family members, is treason to those who did not invite this outside person to come in.

Sabotage comes from the inside.

Sabotage – It can cripple you.

  - It comes from those close to us.

    - It is working in a way as to slow up production or injure the quality of the product.

      - It is a deliberate act of destruction or obstruction.

Examples:

Sabotage comes from the French root word 'sabot' which is the word for shoe or wooden shoe. As the story goes, back in the industrial revolution days when workers had no rights and were commonly misused, overworked, and mistreated, a factory worker would take off a shoe and throw it into the gears to make the gears jam and stop the machine (sabot'age).

A different story comes from Holland where the feudal system was practiced. Feudalism had large land owners and peasants called surfs who, in essence, belonged to the land. They came with the land. It was also a time when tulips (the flower) were used as money. Sometimes the 'Lord of the Manor' would abuse the surfs or maybe take someone's daughter. To get justice, surfs could start stomping on the tulips (sabot'age). Oops! A whole field of tulips/money is destroyed. These examples suggest that some form of provocation triggers sabotage but that's not necessarily so. A reckless or negligent spouse or child who, without provocation, runs up debt on a credit card or gets drunk and wrecks the family car has also committed a very avoidable act of sabotage.

Collusion comes from the inside.

Collusion – It weakens structural integrity.

-It is toxic and corrosive.

-It erodes and undermines the foundation over time,

-It is to conspire in fraud.

-It is to work in concert with…

- It can be done by 'commission,' an active participant.

- It can be done by 'omission' a passive participant, one who goes along, one who sees and says nothing… To quote Robert Kiyosaki, "the silent kiss of death" People are not always consciously aware of their involvement.

Examples:

While securing from within, collusion is the hardest to detect because you have to look at yourself in the process. Examples of collusion by commission are easy: Who can take the most (goods, money, time), make the most personal calls, check email/face book, or gossip while working? It's easy to hold yourself blameless. Treason and sabotage can be done alone but collusion needs at least a tacit (unspoken or implied) tolerance or agreement.

Collusion needs an enabler. If you did not cause harm but allowed or knew of harm being done, did you collude by omission? Hmmh. What are you doing that you don't want to do in order to not offend someone else? What is it that you know and are pretending not to know? What is it that you are pretending to know and really don't know?

You can ask any soldier, policeman, fireman, or even the president. To secure the perimeter and keep harm away from your people is always Job # 1.

Parts of the definitions come from the dictionary; parts from other sources, parts are my own.

*****

You're Committing Treason On Us

I used to own retail shops in shopping malls. All of my employees were young people between 17 and 23 years old. I had a very specific way of hiring people. It had become a ritual that included a series of hurtles to be jumped. A failure to perform any one of them would eliminate you from becoming one of us. The hurdles included:

A four hour interview with me (which included this piece on treason, sabotage, and collusion); interviews with several current employees; quizzing my veterans on what they had learned in their interview with me; reading a book; written book reports, dressing a certain way; etc. It was a tough process. We called it '*Running the gauntlet.*' It's something that everyone went through. They all had commonality of experiences, an instilled vision of what it means, and who they have to become to be a part of our team. They couldn't just want a job. They had to want to be one of us or why go through it.

Years before I started that business I lived in another state and had good friends I had known for years. One of those friends called me and told me he was going through a divorce, had lost his job, and things just weren't going well for him. He asked if he could work for me. This was my good friend. We had been in the trenches together. I knew his whole family, his kids, on and on. I bought him a ticket and told him to come.

Because we had gone through so much together and I knew him to be a good man I thought I could train him and let him supervise my operation. We were in malls that were open 12 hours a day, seven days a week, 361 days a year. My employees made my life tremendously better by relieving me of some of those hours. Before them, if I only worked eight hours on a Sunday it felt like a vacation day.

Anyway, I sent for my friend and put him through the drill. I thought it would be fine. But very soon different members of my team would come to me complaining about how he worked, how he treated them, and his general lack of understanding of what was important to us and how we did things. In other words, he didn't understand or fit into the culture of our business. But for me, I thought when he was there I didn't have to be there. I could get some sleep, make runs, or just take a breath.

Finally after about two weeks of this, one of my team members, Nicole, came and found me. Sometimes she was a little reckless, very emotional, cocky, and loud. You could hear her laughing way down the hallway. But when she was on her stride, she was a whirlwind and a joy to work with. She was smart, intuitive, funny, and dedicated to our system. When she got hired I knew she would be a great leader one day.

She began to tell me about how things were going and the drop in morale on the team. They hated working with him. I listened and then asked her to give it some time. She looked at me directly in my eyes totally exasperated and said, *"You don't understand. You're giving aid and comfort to the enemy. You're committing treason on us!"* She delivered a point blank, bull's eye, arrow to my heart.

I fired my friend the next day and apologized to each member of my team directly. It still stings when I think about that moment. That was a powerful lesson for me. I was like the parent who allowed someone into our home who then mistreated other family members. It was right for her to call me on it. Thank you for your courage and your honesty Nicole. I'll never forget you.

P.S. The essence of this teaching was internalized by Nicole Banks of Milwaukee. She's probably in her early forties now in 2015. I don't know how to reach her. But this is a gesture of respect to her.

*****

Securing the Perimeter

I had left Illinois on my way to Austin, Texas. It's a 1,200 mile ride. I stopped in Oklahoma City and spent a day with a very good friend. We grew up together a block apart. I left in the morning.

I arrived in Dallas, Texas later that afternoon and stopped to see one of my favorite cousins, his sister, and my uncle. They lived in a marginal apartment complex in a not so good part of town. We had a great time catching up and she made a fantastic home cooked dinner.

My uncle was a veteran of the Korean War and man of few words although he would lighten up around other adult family members. Growing up when I'd drop by he would have his music on, a cigarette, and maybe a drink. He wasn't mean but always seemed thoughtful and very serious. He didn't miss much. My aunt had died when we were little and left him with 4 small children to raise. They had it rough but you could tell he did the best he could by all of us. This one particular night he was happier than I had ever seen him, laughing and telling us stories about my parents, their parents, and other people we knew. His children were all grown now. He had grandchildren, and the weight of the world was off of his shoulders.

I wanted to be in Austin in the morning. It was a weekday. They couldn't stay up all night talking to me. They had to go to work. So rather than wake them up in the middle of the night I decided to catch a few hours of sleep in my pickup truck. It was parked in the lot across from their apartment. Then I could a leave whenever I felt rested. I woke up about 3:00 in the morning. I sat up, got the sleep out of my eyes and started up my truck. I looked over at my cousins' door. My uncle was standing in the doorway smoking a cigarette, watching me. Like a good soldier he was securing the perimeter, keeping harm away from his people. But he was bigger than that to me. He was a guardian angel. He had been there all night. I waved, and he waved as I pulled off. That's the last time I ever saw him. What a phenomenal demonstration. To this very day, I have never felt so safe and protected in my whole entire life.

Job # 1. Secure the perimeter. Keep harm away from your people.

Book Four

Family

They're always with us and us with them.

Fathers
(Letter to My Nephews)

Hello family… Happy Father's day!!!

When you say you're a man, a husband, or a father, you've said a mouth full. Being a son, brother, uncle, or nephew are special relationships as well but that's for another day.

All of you have young ones in your care. They help to make the world make sense. '*This is why I go to work. This is why I bought this house. This is why I put up with…*' They let you know that there are other important things in the world than your little stuff. They're good at that. They come from us but are not of us. They are God's children, as are you, and they belong to the future. We just get a chance to hold them, mold them, and keep them for a while. Be their father while they grow up. Maybe you can be their friend later.

Teach them well. They will hear your voice in their heads for the rest of their lives. Make sure what they hear from you is good, strong, just, and wise. Be clear about this point, you are the example. They will look to you and learn from you for the kind of person they want to be, or not be. Treat them with care and compassion. Remember that one day you will need them more than they need you.

Some of us are natural fathers. Others of us are natural husbands. Keep in mind that children will grow up and leave. But hopefully your wife will still be there. Do not put your children before your wife or allow her to do so. If you and mom are on one accord the kids will be okay.

Be sure to leave your children with the good name that you were given. It will mean much to them later.

Teach them how to worship God. They need to have a system of morality and ethics to guide them. There will be times when the world turns upside down and they won't know what to do or how to proceed. To know that God loves His children and He hears your prayers, that He is merciful, a healer, and the giver of grace, will be a great comfort to them.

Teach them the benefits of cooperation, to do things together, to support, and to show up for each other. How do you know who's on your team? Who can you call? Who shows up? After all, their relationships with each other are the longest relationships they ever will have. It will be a relief to them to be able to call on each other long after you may be gone.

Teach them about responsibility, work, and contributing to the home. No I'm not paying you for helping around the house. You live here. Here is what I tried to do with varying degrees of success:

By three or four years old they can pick up their room, and sweep the kitchen. By age five they can empty the trash, and stand on a chair and do the dishes. At six they open a bank account. By ten they could garden and clean everything – kitchen, bathrooms, laundry, windows, etc. By 12 they could cook a 5-course dinner. By 15 tell them to start looking for loans, grants, and scholarships because you may not be paying for college. They already know how expensive it is. Actually I would pay as best I could like everybody else. It's amazing how creative and resourceful children can be. They will love you for what you do for them. They will be stronger for what you do not do for them.

Teach them to be kind, respectful, and considerate to other people. They need to know that the world does not revolve around them and that it's nice to be nice. They may or may not be recognized for these traits right away. But those with a bad attitude are always easy to recognize all around the world.

Teach them about their culture so they can be proud of who they are, where they're from, and the contributions of their ancestors. This acts as an anchor and gives them a sense of their special place the world.

Teach them to manage their resources, their time, money, and talents, so they can maximize their assets whatever they may be. You will see their gifts, talents, and character traits long before they do. It could be intellectual, physical, musical, financial, spiritual, mechanical, etc. Help them to recognize and express them because they may not see it. To the person with the gift or talent it's no big deal. They think their exceptional gift is normal. They're just being who they are. This helps them develop a sense of responsibility and self-worth. They need to know how to make wise choices. You want them to be able to take care of themselves, possibly others, and maybe even you.

Teach them manners. Good manners can give them an advantage in school, in society, at work, and maybe keep them out of trouble with the law. It doesn't just make then look good. It reflects on you. Sometimes they will ignore their good home training but once instilled, it never goes away. No one wants to put up with other people's bad behavior. It's hard for people to hear you when they can't get past your lack of social graces. Your children may be precious to you but they will be accepted or excluded largely by how they interact with others.

Allow them to make mistakes. It's hard for a parent to watch because you can see mistakes coming. Resist the urge to do their homework, finish a project for them, or come behind them and fix their mistakes. They need to know that disappointment will visit their lives. In the real world everybody doesn't get a trophy. They need to know there are consequences both good and bad. Yet, inside of those disappointments are always lessons to be learned and sometimes opportunity. Sometimes we're on the winning team. Sometimes we're on the learning team. Make sure they know how they messed up. Help them get the lesson rather than merely punish them. Make sure they know the difference between: I did a bad thing verses I'm a bad person. Mistakes don't make you a bad person. Everybody makes mistakes. Sometimes I think my biggest asset is that I've made so many mistakes that I'm pretty good at it. I can see them coming or I can get up quickly.

Teach them that sometimes an apology is in order and to have the honorable character and humility to give one. The ability to say, *"I'm sorry I was wrong, excuse me, or forgive me,"* doesn't make you appear smaller. Not being able to does. Most people can accept a sincere apology. What they can't take is a cover up or a lack of acknowledgement that harm was done. Teach them to think, reflect, and make the correction. You want your children to become wise.

Remember, your children don't listen to what you say. They look at who you are and they do that. They don't care about the money you spend on them. They care about the time you spend with them.

If you will patiently demonstrate these lessons, you will raise fantastic citizens for the whole world. And if they never get into honors geometry, it's okay.

God bless you and your family.

Manners

I grew up with a house full of children. It's untenable to have even one unruly child in your home much less a house full of them. Every day we would have manners reminders dropped on us. They were ubiquitous in our home. My mother would say, *"You better mind your manners. Don't embarrass your family."*

My mother had a little safety pin somewhere on her person at all times. In my whole life I never saw it. But whether she was nicely dressed or in her house clothes, you could bet she had that safety pin with her somewhere. So if you ignored your grammar or your manners, you might get stuck with that pin. She was amazingly quick on the draw. *"Ouch!"* I must have gotten stuck a thousand times with that thing.

My mother would say, *"Graciousness is the lubrication of civilization."* So even as a teenager when I was screwing up terribly, I still had great manners. *"Will you pass that cigarette please?"*

Here's a rundown of what we got on a regular basis:

"Please. Thank you. Excuse me. Yes sir. No ma'am,. Hold your head up. Walk like you're going somewhere. Look people in the eye when you talk to them. Shake people's hands firmly. Clean up what you mess up. Respect everyone, especially your elders. Sit up straight. Stand up straight. Don't talk with your mouth full. Take your hat off in the house. Take your elbows off the table. Walk on the outside. Open the door for that lady. Give that lady your seat. Wear clean underwear in case you're in an accident."

Here's another one: *If a task is once begun do not stop until it's done. Be the labor great or small, do your best or not at all."* (Quote Walberg Schools)

Even though it seemed annoying at the time, these rules and principles have served me far better, around the world, than all the formal education I've acquired through the years. People everywhere want to be treated with respect. They value their families. They want to eat well and have decent housing, whatever that means. They want meaningful work. They want to be accepted by their group, their peers, their people. An act of kindness, a word of encouragement, or a friendly smile translates all over the world.

After returning from one place or another people will often ask, *"How is it over there?"*

I then ask them, *"How is it where you are?"*

I do this because I know, if you're a kind and respectful person here, those are generally the people you'll meet wherever you go. Arrogant, selfish, judgmental, or inconsiderate people are easily recognized everywhere and treated accordingly.

"Mind your manners. Don't embarrass your family."

'Graciousness really is the lubrication of civilization.'

Bankroll Kids

She was six year old when I told her it was time for her to take care of her own money. I would start giving her five dollars a week with conditions.

First, she would have to come to the bank with me every week and put two dollars in the bank for twelve straight weeks. If she did that, I would double her money in the bank. So $24.00 would then become $48.00.

Second, give one dollar away to someone less fortunate than herself or to a 'do-gooder' cause. Give to church, food pantries, local nonprofits, etc.

Third, you have two dollars to spend as you wish.

By the time they're six years old they're very good at asking for things they want. That's a good time to start teaching responsibility around money. They also make reasonable associations about money from their point of view such as:

*You, the parent are supposed to buy them whatever they want or need.
*Credit cards and check books = money. So if you have a check book or a credit card, you must have money.
*If you go to work, you must have money.
*They should have what all the other kids have.
*They cannot pay (for whatever it is).
*They shouldn't have to pay (for whatever it is) even if they have the money.

It was time to take her to the bank. While in the parking lot I told her there are three basic concepts she needed to know before we open a savings account. We sat in the parking lot for about 20 minutes until she could recite these three concepts by heart. The problem with teaching them is that the wisdom you teach the kids can come back to bite you.

1. Save ten percent (10%) of your income first. In other words, take your savings out right off the top. That's before you eat, pay a bill, or whatever other things you want or need to do. That is for savings. If you do this systematically, in 10 pay periods you have saved 1 whole pay amount.

2. The key to having money is to keep some in reserve. Spend less than you make. Just because you have money doesn't mean you have to spend it.

3.Never pay retail. That's why God made consumers.

(Lesson for me) This one came back to bite me in a huge way decades later.

So before you buy something you can ask yourself:
Is this a want, a need, or a demand (A demand is a want with the ability to pay for it, recreate it, or do without it).

The first couple of 12 week cycles, she came every time. It's not unusual for the kids to want to be with you anyway. Plus they understand and like that their money is getting doubled. The third cycle she only came 9 times. I did not double her money. So imagine a little snag-a-tooth six year old saying, *"Daddy, you may not have meant to but I think you cheated me."*

(Lesson for her): *"No I did not cheat you. I kept my agreement. You did not keep your agreement by coming 12 straight weeks. How do you build trust? You make small agreements and you keep them."*

*(Here's the bite for me): For the rest of their lives when they want something, and I say yes or maybe, they ask for an agreement from me. Ouch.

(Lesson for me): Later, at nine or ten years old you start to hear things like; All I want is... Everybody's got this... I'm the only one who doesn't have..., can't go..., or has to...

One day she came to me and said, *"Dad."*

I'm thinking, *"Uh Oh. I know that voice and that look. She's going to ask me for something."*

"Everybody's got these kinds of blue jeans but me. I'm the only one who doesn't ..."

"How much do they cost?"

"Eighty Dollars."

I said, *"Eighty dollars for some blue jeans? Okay. No problem. I'll give you $20. You have money. Spend your own money."*

Her answer, *"NOOOO!"*

*(Here's the bite for her): Then she learned about value. Not only know how much something cost, but also know how much it is worth to me. That's a value question.

She's married now with a couple of kids. She came to me a few years ago and said, *"Dad."*

I'm thinking, *"Uh Oh. I know that voice and that look. She's going to ask me for something."*

"I just found the perfect house for my family. It has vaulted ceilings, a kitchen island, granite counter tops, tile here, hardwood there, master bed, bath, etc. Will you help me put a down payment on the house?"

"Nope, not a nickel, you have a husband. Let him buy you a house. If you had come to me about a two flat or a four unit with

renters that could help you pay for the house, then we could have a conversation."

"My bad."

*(Here's the bite for me): Two or three months later she came back to me and said, "Dad."

I'm thinking, "Oh Oh. I know that voice and that look. She's going to ask me for something."

"I just found another house."

I gave her the side eye and literally growl at her.

"The lot is 1/3 bigger than all the other lots around there. I talked him down from this price to a 20% lower price. And I got the financing 2 points lower than the going rate. I didn't pay retail dad. I didn't. I didn't."

When I looked in her face, all I could see was the snag-a-tooth six year old. She got me for five figures that day.

The point is to raise wise, self-sufficient children who are smart with their money. But be careful. It can come back to bite you.

Book Five

Business

How you think and feel about money can make you rich... or not!

What Is Money

Money! I am writing this because on countless occasions I have freely and carelessly thrown this word around thinking that I knew what money is and what I was talking about. I was incredibly wrong. It cost me and millions of other people dearly on a daily basis. I felt the sting of losing everything twice. It forced me to question what I really know about money and to ultimately ask the question, *"What is money?"*

Money is an idea, representing work truly done, backed by the confidence that someone will except it for what you say it's worth, and it is exchangeable.

Money is a medium of exchange, a medium of trade. If what is considered money does not have all of these features represented, it is not money.

Money is an idea.

It is a concept, a thought that represents a universally accepted gesture of what value is in a given culture. Value is the key because value indicates worth in the eyes of the beholder. The value question is, *'What is it worth to me'* (whatever it is)? In every society and in every subculture of any society there is a concept of money. Money can be represented by the actual unit or object of trade (a cow). Or it can be represented by a facsimile (a paper dollar). Or it can be represented by something universally accepted as valuable such as gold or silver. The actual unit or the facsimile or the accepted valuable item could all be considered currency. In most cases the greater the beauty, rarity, exclusivity, creativity, meaning, or desire for it, the greater the value. *If the 'currency' does not have the perception/idea of value, it is not money.*

Money represents work truly done.

What gives money value is the 'work' that went into the objects of value. Some ways of looking at 'work truly done' are: creating (art or inventions), growing (food), finding (jewels, metals, oil), processing (refining), harnessing power: (water, wind, geothermal, solar), building, thinking, innovating (new ways of doing or new uses), etc., the objects of value. There must be a real value added.

Let's make a finer distinction with an analogy.

Let us say you take a class in school and receive an A for a grade. It is assumed that you have (to a high degree) come to class regularly, listened to the lecture and read the corresponding text, done the homework, taken the tests, understood the questions, and answered appropriately and accurately on multiple occasions. And, later you could take that accumulated knowledge and transfer it into useful work or understanding in the field over time. The A does in fact represent work truly done.

Can a person cheat and get an A in the class? Yes. If getting the A came by cheating, can the person transfer what they know about the class into useful work in the field? No. The knowledge must be actually acquired. There must be an assumption that it could really be applied at some point in the future. Without the work truly done, the A has no meaning. It is not an A.

If the US government wanted to generate more cash flow for the country, could someone put in an order to Fort Knox to print up an additional million dollars? Yes. Would that currency hold the same value as the previous money in circulation? No. It would just be paper with printing on it. It would not be backed by any increase in production, trade, or any added value anywhere. It would not represent work truly done. If it did, every country on the globe would just print more money. There would be no poor countries.

In the Weimar Republic, Germany in the 1930's, printing money is exactly what they did. And shortly thereafter, when citizens got paid, they would literally have to hurry to the bank with wheelbarrows, load up with cash, and then run to the store before the money lost any more value.

What would happen if you showed up for work but didn't do anything? Would that be okay? Do you think any employer could afford that over time? Would you expect to be paid?

Money represents an idea of something for something. *If it does not represent 'work truly done,' it is not money.*

Money is backed by the confidence that someone will accept it for what you say it's worth.

Worth indicates the upper limit of what someone will pay in price or terms. Gold is worth X amount per ounce right now. It is agreed upon around the world every day. Value is more subjective. The value question is, '*What is it worth to me?*'(whatever 'it' is). When the world is generally a peace and there is a high level of certainty, the price of gold goes down. During times of war, natural disasters, and general uncertainty, the price of gold goes up. Worth can stand alone on a large scale. Value determines worth to the individual. Worth will adjust to fit value. No one will pay more than how much they value something. After that value is exceeded, people exercise another option: to do without/and or find another alternative. If enough people decide to or are forced to do without or find another alternative the worth drops and a new worth is established. Monetary worth is determined by the confidence and willingness of someone else to accept what you say it's worth. It must be agreed upon.

Let's say you are in the USA and you want to sell a chair for $100. Someone then offers you $100 dollars for the chair but they offer $100 in Canadian money as payment. Would you accept it as payment? The short answer is no. Why? Because the odds are you don't know what $100 dollars Canadian is worth in USA dollars. You don't know whether its' buying power/value is worth more or less than $100 USA. You don't know if it's a good deal. It is prudent to say no. You know its currency. It's legal tender worth $100 in Canada. But at the point where you do not have the confidence to accept it as payment, it is not money.

In the late 1990's, the price of internet dot com stocks was very high. The problem was most of them were not generating a profit for investors. Investors did not feel like they were getting their 'money's worth'. The price was too high. The confidence in their value went down. The bubble had to burst. The stocks became 'worth less.' A new worth was established. In 2008 it was a real estate bubble that burst.

In the Montgomery, Alabama bus boycott in the 1950's, Rosa Parks (one individual) decided there was only one way a bus ride would be worth it to her. After paying full fare, she would have to be able to sit anywhere she wanted. She did not want to have to sit at the back of the bus. The terms or price was too high. There was no agreement with the bus company or Southern society on this issue. She was arrested. Apparently Black people all over town agreed with her. Black people refused to ride the busses for over a year (a willingness to do without) at no small hardship to themselves. They exercised another option. They found another alternative. With the loss of huge numbers of riders the value of the bus company dropped which made it 'worth less.' The company ultimately went out of business. A new worth was established for ridership on Montgomery busses. The terms were changed.

To me, it seems like that would have been a great time for one or more of those Black riders to become owners of the bus company thus creating real wealth in their community. But that's another story.

Monetary worth is determined by the confidence and willingness of someone else to accept something for what you say it's worth. Without the confidence, it is not money.

Money is exchangeable.
Money is a medium of exchange. In other words, you can trade money with someone for an item you want to purchase. That person can then take the money he received from you and trade it with someone else for something else. That demonstrates that the money was exchangeable.

One night after partying like there was no tomorrow, I made my way to an all-night diner in the wee hours of the morning. I happened to find myself in a family style seating arrangement in the presence of several other late night people including a 'working woman of the night.' I know how this may sound but I'm innocent of any further implication. All of us just had a conversation. That's all. We were not having a business conversation but the topic of money did come up. At one point in the conversation she said, "*I always have money because I'm sitting on my money.*" Later, I thought about what she said and scrutinized the validity of her comment.

Can 'her money' represent an idea of something of value to someone else? Yes. Can it represent something for which work is truly done? Yes. Could someone accept it for what she says it's worth? Yes. Is it exchangeable? In other words, can someone receive what she is exchanging and then later, exchange it for something else? No. It's not money.

If you cannot exchange it once, and then again, it is not money.

*****

Money can come in different forms. We normally think of money in the form of paper currency, gold, silver, and recently even bit coins. However, if you are in a war-torn region, what is money? Why or for what would someone be willing trade very precious items?

- What do the fortunate or those in power have that the weaker don't have? Arms.
- If you are in a famine-stricken region, what is money? Food.
- If you are in a desert, what is money? Water.
- If you are in a drug-infested area, what is money? Drugs.
- A couple of centuries ago in Holland it was tulips.
- A couple of centuries ago in the Caribbean it was rum.

The examples over time and place are endless.

Summary

On a personal level, pay attention to your behavior with money. All money does is make you more of what you already are. If you're frugal, generous, very social, an introvert, a saver, an investor, money will make you more of that. A fool and his money will soon be parted anyway. That never changes.

Why is this important? In a time when trade is global, when goodwill and admiration from much of the world has left our shores, when whole economies can rise and fall in short order, when over 1/4 of the world's population live on less than $3.00 a day; when our dollar is no longer backed by gold or silver but by purple mountains majesty, when our country is trillions of dollars in debt to those who would harm us, when our country has become the greatest debtor nation in the history of mankind, when six in ten of our citizens are in debt personally, it is important to know what money is and how to recognize it. At this point in time it may be wise to ask the question, *'What is money?'*

What Is Welfare

My records were meticulous. I could tell you how much money we made on the second Tuesday of the month, every month, for three years. I owned retail shops in malls and I knew exactly what to expect. There was a young lady who worked as the manager of a shop in the mall who wanted to work with us. She'd come by all the time. We had to let a few people go so we gave her a chance. She went through the training, worked with us directly, and had a great attitude. It seemed to be workings out.

Finally we gave her the responsibility to run the shop for a few weeks. It was a good opportunity for her and it gave me a break from the day-to-day operation. Our numbers plummeted. We were down by over 60% every time she was there. I checked the inventory. She wasn't stealing. I had checked her references and had seen her work before in another place. She was competent. I reviewed the training. I had part-timers doing a way better job than she was. I even stepped in to help her for another couple of days. The numbers recovered. It was hard to figure out at first.

Then came payday. We had to have a talk about her performance. That's when it became clear. She felt like if she showed up and put in the hours, then she did her job and wanted to be paid like she had done something special. She felt entitled to be paid for exceptional or at least acceptable work. I did pay her but I paid with resentment. Then cut her loose. I couldn't afford her. Nobody could.

First, what do you call it when people feel entitled to be paid for work not truly done? She wasn't even trying to do better. Second, what is it called when you pay for work not truly done, but pay with resentment?

What is that?

Welfare!

The only difference between her and those on public aid is that those on public aid actually know they're on welfare. And most of them really do need some kind of assistance. She did not. It would express a lack of human compassion not to assist those who really need it. That's a different situation. I don't know if she ever got the lesson. But I sure did.

Why Get A Job & What You Get
(Western Industrial Vs. Hunter Gatherer Society)

In America we hear this refrain the whole time we're growing up: *"Get a good education. Get a good job."*

Indeed, there are some very good reasons to get a job.

Someone will pay you to teach or train you. Someone else is willing to absorb your mistakes and still pay you. You can actually get a pass or a jump start until your learning curve gets up to speed. You can feel like part of a team and belong to something bigger than yourself. When you work for yourself, if you make a mistake you pay the toll. You basically cast your bread upon the water, work hard, and wait for it to come back. You start at a deficit and try to get back to zero. When you get back to 'break even,' you have a big party to celebrate not losing money.

You can get benefits like: health insurance, vacation time, parental leave, or a pension. They will pay to keep you healthy and pay you when you're sick. There are 401k plans where they give you free money if you save some for yourself, etc.

You can make contacts with people who have skills and insights that you may find useful later.

There is usually a gap between what is needed, what is wanted, and what is being done. Sometimes there are whole unexplored avenues that no one ever thought about. When you do something every day you begin to see the gap. You can figure out how to do things more efficiently or effectively. In that gap there is opportunity, or niche.

Entrepreneurs are born in that gap. The gap is the seed for ideas that you might be able to grow or express later. The gap is where innovation lives. Innovation is the wildcard in supply and demand where fortunes are made or lost. Startup businesses, exploration, research and development, and new enterprises live in that innovation gap.

Smart employers will ask their employees what they think and listen attentively to the answers. Good employers will publicly acknowledge and reward them for good suggestions.

You can take the time to design your life and still get a regular check.

You can save your money and buy your freedom like the slaves did in the past.

If you love what you do, if you would consider doing it for free and someone will actually pay you for it anyway, that's fantastic. That's not work. That's paradise.

There are also very good reasons not to get a job.

It's hard to win because the rules are not designed for you to win. The rules are designed for owners, board members, and stock holders to win. Generally employers will pay a competitive wage that's just enough to keep you from quitting.

It's hard to break even because someone else tells you when to come and go, how much you earn, where you can live (based on income), when and where you take vacations (related to earnings and their busy season), who your team is, what your purpose is, and if you are going to take another step up on the ladder, someone else tells you which ladder – how many steps up you can take – and what wall you will be leaning on.

It's hard to get out of the game because of the accumulation of expenses and debt: house - cars – children – credit cards – school loans – unexpected and/or persistent medical expenses - insurance coverage – etc.

I think most of us would agree that a regular steady paycheck can provide a reassuring level of comfort. The huge drawback is that it can imperceptibly slip golden handcuffs on your life. Without noticing you begin to adjust your life to fit your paycheck instead of adjusting your life to fit your dreams. *"A steady paycheck can knock the hustle out of you."* (Wilson, Kye)

What if you get sick or hurt, your car breaks down, or you have to move? Does the job understand that life happens while you're planning other stuff?

Time is another issue. A big problem with most full-time jobs is they want you to be there all the time, be on call, answer a zillion work-related messages, and generally put their priorities first. Don't take too many vacation days, personal days, or parental leave. Don't even mention your elderly parents or a disabled sibling or relative. There are a lot of single people and divorced people. What about having a little time to establish a personal relationship with someone? Any time for that? What if a spouse or child gets sick? What about their school plays, sports events, or parent-teacher conferences? Children remember who shows up for them their whole lives. Where do children go and what are they doing when they get out of school? Is anybody home? Can you get there? What are you supposed to do? Unless you work for yourself can you take your family where you go and teach them what you know? Your family is normally not welcome on the job. Don't spend too much time talking to or messaging them either. The very people you are really working for are the ones you may not be able to spend much time with. It can be a real issue. After working as much as you do, do you have the time and/or energy to enjoy, create, or manifest your ideal life?

There are certainly rewards to having steady employment. Just be sure to measure the cost.

*****

Hunter Gatherer

I was watching an educational program about the characteristics of different kinds of societies and how it relates to the culture. There are:

Western Industrial societies (like America or Germany), Theocracies (like Israel or Iran), Monarchies (like England, Spain, or Saudi Arabia), Military (where the army runs everything), Kleptocracies (whoever can steal the most from their own people or other countries has the power - every continent), Agrarian (agriculture based economies), Tribal (where tribes, clans, and ethnicity dominate the socio-political landscape), Nomadic Herders (cultures that herd cattle, sheep, reindeer, etc.) Hunter Gathers (cultures that hunt, fish, and live off the fat of the land - from the arctic to the rainforest), etc.

Let me say that each kind of culture is special in its' own way and each incorporated aspects that other cultures could benefit from. It is not my intent to be in judgment. I am attempting to be objective.

At one end of the spectrum are the industrial western societies. At the other end are the hunter gather societies. So let's take a closer look.

A major characteristic of *hunter gather societies* is they basically forage far and wide in the landscape to get what they need to meet their necessities. They know what they are looking for and how to find it. The catch is, will it be there when they need/want it.

Another major feature is their cooperative, interdependent relationships with their families and other members of their group. Family is very important. Everyone's assets are valued and there is extremely little waste of energy or resources. Exchange is direct, clear, and proportional. Everyone knows why they do what they do and the impact it has.

A major problem is they are at the mercy of the elements and more powerful groups, either of which can put them in serious peril. Life can be hard but not lonely or without meaning.

A major benefit is that you as a person are important. No one is expendable. People are clear about why they live as they do. There is no conflict on what is important to them. Their wealth is in their relationships, their community, knowledge of the environment, and conservation of resources. They have each other. When things go well or adversely, they know why.

From my point of view, most Americans would not think of this as a desirable alternative.

A major characteristic of **western industrialized societies** is they forage far and wide in the market place for a job to get what they need to meet their necessities. They don't necessarily know what they are looking for or how to find it. The catch is, will it be there when they need/want it. It's the same catch as hunter gatherers.

Another major feature is that they have almost optionally cooperative and optionally interdependent relationships with their families and other members of their group. However, it is almost required that they have cooperative/competitive relationships on the job. Everyone's assets are not necessarily valued at home or on the job. There can easily be a tremendous waste of energy and resources. Exchange is indirect. Money is the medium of exchange for work done, not a cow. It's not always clear (a lot of people don't know why they are useful), and generally not proportional in terms of time, effort, and income. Look at how much the CEO makes as opposed to other people although we usually agree to the terms. It's part of our culture. There can easily be a detachment between what we do and the impact it has.

A major benefit is their standard of living can largely be self-directed. Life can be exceptionally good. Family and group relationships can be maintained and/or developed.

A major problem is that you as a person may or may not be important. You may be expendable. You are at the mercy of the overall economy, the job market in your geographic location or your field of expertise, and more powerful groups, any of which can put you in serious peril. It is easy to have a huge disconnect with your family and your group. A lot of people can fall through the cracks individually, as large populations, or whole industries in mass. Life can be hard and lonely.

From my point of view, most hunter gatherers would not think of this as a desirable alternative.

With all of the good that comes from each kind of culture, there is much to be questioned about both as far as the quality of life is concerned.

*****

The paradox is:

It is my opinion that in our western industrialized society, we have become and are teaching our children to become hunter gatherers for jobs instead of foragers for our ideal lives. "*I just want to be comfortable.*" or "*I get in where I fit in.*" is a common refrain. "*I'm getting by. I'm surviving.*" and "*I'm doing okay.*" are the new fantastic. We tend to work and educate ourselves and our children to not be poor as opposed to thrive, to cooperate with each other, and/or use our one natural gifts and talents to live our ideal lives.

Considering that all of us have issues and challenges, then normal is not bad if your life is working for you. Indeed, if you don't mind getting up and facing it every day, and you're not doing a swirly down the drain, then I agree. That's kind of fantastic. It's a matter of perspective.

What is your hearts' desire? Are you clear about it? Do you plan for it? Are you making room to receive it? And can you get there from the path you're on now?

Maybe I'm a dreamer but I believe that every good thing we ever wanted is in the realm of possibility.

The Power Principle

In the ***beginning*** you have an idea about what you would like or how to make things better with a business.

Emotion: The emotion is optimism.

Action: The appropriate action is to begin.

Emergency is what comes up immediately. Everything you don't know pops up in your face. *"The principles reveal themselves upon the decision."* (Buckminster Fuller)

Emotion: The emotion that comes up is fear, doubt or panic.

Action: What most people will do is get cautious and stick their toe in the water.

What they should do is promote, promote, promote like crazy.

Normal is the next stage. It is a slow steady rise. Things are moving along. Progress is being made.

Emotion: The emotion that comes up is boredom.

Action: The action a lot of people take is to create drama because they feel like they are going in slow motion and what they are doing is mundane. What they should do is continue doing what they're doing. It's working. Progress is being made.

Affluence is the next stage. That's when you get a sharp spike up in business and money starts pouring in.

Emotion: The emotion that comes up is greed. They've got a pocket full of money and their eyes get big.

Action: People start to conspicuously consume. They buy the Rolex, the expensive cars, the clothes and jewelry, the international trips, the way bigger home, or even the getaway home.
What they should do is pay off debts, cut back, save, invest, and diversify.

Power is reached when you can walk away for six months to a year or more with little to no involvement in the business without a loss in income. You have effectively replaced yourself.

Then do it again.

All credit goes to Robert Kiyosaki who discussed this principle with me.

Wealth

I'm going to ask you to take a stretch of consciousness right up front. God makes too much of everything we need to prosper in abundance. Abundance and scarcity co-exist. They are flip sides of the same coin. Every day we make a choice. Most of us get in our own way. What we usually lack is some combination of courage, commitment, creativity, curiosity, and/or cooperation. Most of all we lack a compelling purpose and the faith that we can actually have the life we want. If you try, you may or may not reap the benefits. At the very least, you can learn to plant the seeds of wealth. If you don't try, you always pay the toll.

In 1990 I lost tens of thousands of dollars in sixty days doing big money business with some millionaire guys. I'm talking about liquid cash, my money. It was all legal, moral, and ethical but they ate my lunch. I thought I was smart. I thought I knew what I was doing but it became painfully clear that I was being confronted with my ignorance.

Mistakes are God's way of putting what we don't know right in our face. I grew up with no money. We had a house, a car and a dog but no money. I remember the first time I took a bath by myself, slept in a bed by myself, and the first pair of pants that belonged to me, green corduroy pants. I was number five of six boys growing up so I always got the hand me downs.

By the 1990's I had already been homeless twice so I hated losing money. You have to either have, or be making good money just to lose that much money. I was devastated. This loss hurt my whole spirit. Even worse than losing the money and being broke for a while, was not knowing what happened.

I had to ask myself very fundamental questions such as, what is money, wealth, an investment, credit, debt, an asset, a liability, stock, etc. I knew I had to learn because I was not willing to go through this again. You can pay for a good education one time but you pay for ignorance over and over again. Ignorance is expensive.

I began a quest to find out what happened to my money. As we all know, when the student is ready, the teacher appears.

After a few months one of the millionaires called me. He said, *"Sometimes the bulls win. Sometimes the bears win. But the pigs always get slaughtered. You were the pig. We took your money. It wasn't a personal matter. We're millionaires. Making money is what we do. There are very few young guys (I was in my thirties) and no Black guys out here. But we like you. You've got balls. We'll teach you. We'll charge you but we'll teach you."*

That was an offer I couldn't refuse. The cost was not my concern. It couldn't cost more than my ignorance. All I wanted to know was what to do next. *"The principles reveal themselves upon the commitment."* (Kiyosaki, Robert) When you commit, everything you don't know pops up in your face immediately. Thankfully, I had no idea what I was in for.

I took over fifteen seminars, each one taught by masters. There were five real estate courses taught by people who bought and sold hundreds of properties each, a class on stocks and bonds taught by a man who had made over a billion dollars in deals on Wall Street – over 200- million plus dollar deals. I walked on hot coals with my bare feet to learn how to focus. I climbed up and stood on the top of a tree trunk the diameter of a saucer, forty feet in the air, then jumped to a trapeze to learn the management of fear. The tree didn't stop swaying until I stopped shaking. In another class, a man held an arrow to the soft spot in my neck. I walked into it to get the essence of trust. The arrow bowed and snapped in half. I read over 200 books, listened to 400 tapes in four different countries at a cost of over $100 thousand dollars to find out what happened to my money. I was serious. It was no casual affair. I learned and here are some of the things I found out:

I found out I had been a greedy fat caterpillar eating up all the leaves. It was all about me and mine, what I need, what I like, and what I want. I had started a business with $50 dollars in the bank, no job, no credit, and had built it to four retail shops at the time. I was busy. If I only worked 8 hours on a Sunday it felt like a vacation day. I didn't mean anyone any harm but if I saw a dagger sticking out of your chest, I could step right over you. *"I'll call 911 when I get where I'm going. I gotta' go."* If you were not another merchant, a supplier, an employee, or a customer, I just didn't have time for you, period. I had a bankroll but no life. The tail was wagging the dog.

I found out that Caesar must get his due in taxes and that God must get his due in good will towards men. I wasn't doing enough good will towards men. In either case, if you don't willingly give, it will be taken. That's the short story of why I lost my money.

I started giving ten percent of my income as a defensive measure. It was truly defensive giving. It was a pretty fair nugget I was giving every week. I wanted to be on the good side of God or at least not on his bad side. I didn't want God to lay me flat and take all of my stuff, again. I didn't think of it as sowing and reaping. I just didn't want to be penalized for not giving. It was painful. I hated parting with my money as a something for nothing proposition. In my head I thought of my donations as doing God's work. But in my heart I gave from the point of view of paying protection money to God.

I started giving by making donations to churches, schools, charities, and the food bank. I liked the food bank because they got 14 pounds of food for every one dollar donated. From a greedy fat caterpillar point of view I liked the return on investment (ROI) even though it didn't go to me. I remember thinking, *"I'm really helping these people."* After a short while I realized that my little donations seemed like a lot to me but to the scale of those organizations, and to the vast need, it was a mere drop in the bucked.

Then one day I thought of the Law of Reciprocation.

Christians say, *"Do unto others as you would have them do unto you."*

"Give and it shall be given unto you…"

Jewish people say *"An eye for an eye. A finger for a finger."*

Buddhists say, *"The magnificent Law of Cause and Effect."*

On the street they say, *"What goes around comes around."*

It's the same law. You get what you give. I was making a good bit of money and I was giving that 10% consistently. Then I thought, *"I might have some blessings coming my way."* so I started looking for them. I began to see them all the time, everywhere, in the form of goodwill, opportunity, and sometimes cash. What I realized was I was helping myself. You can have money and still feel poor. Giving helped me to not feel poor. Before, I felt like I couldn't afford to give. I found that I couldn't afford not to give. Now instead of paying protection money to God which was painful, I give until it hurts in a good way. I've become a cheerful giver.

I learned that the physical, spiritual, emotional, intellectual, and financial were all connected. They are all different forms of wealth. And that it's the one category you don't pay attention to that affects all of the others. It is my belief that God expresses himself in all of these and probably more ways, in different people. Some people would call these gifts or talents.

When Michael Jordan slam-dunks in three players faces, that's how he expresses God, in a physical way. When Dear Abby responds to a letter and it hits thousands of readers in their hearts, that's how she expresses God, emotionally. When a teacher squeezes understanding out of a mysterious concept and then sees the light come on in her students, that's her expression of God, intellectually. When an investor puts his money on the line and then watches it come back to him bigger than it left, that's how he expresses God, financially. When a minister delivers a sermon and people come to the alter to be closer to God, that's his expression of God, spiritually.

All of these components are a part of our daily lives and must be paid some attention. All of these can be developed. It is also important to find out as best you can how you express God most efficiently. What are your gifts? Balance is the key. I had been kind of an intellectually creative strong man but a spiritual pencil-neck weakling. I lost what had been important to me. These imbalances can happen in infinite combinations. Just pay attention.

It then came to me that everyone is already smart enough. They already have natural God-given gifts and talents. They have everything they need and more to far exceed whatever expectations they may have for themselves. What I lacked was the ability to recognize and access emotional acumen for lessons such as: desire, commitment, faith, persistence, courage, balance, teamwork, love, trust, integrity, and forgiveness. There are many more emotions both positive and negative as well that any given person may be susceptible to. The point is to recognize them and make an adjustment when they come up. If you don't control your emotions, they will control you. I had to learn how to recognize greed. That was a big one for me.

*****

In 1994 I took a class called: <u>How To Get Rich For World Peace.</u> I was evolving. I figured world peace was a good reason to get rich. I'll take one for the team. It was a ten-day class that started on January 10th and was over on January 19th at a beautiful resort in Hawaii. There were about 110 people from all over the world with only ten Americans. On the 20th, I came down for breakfast early in the morning. The sun was just coming up over the ocean and there was only one other person present. He was one of the students, a mega-millionaire, named Bill. He invited me to sit with him.

He was in a somewhat reflective mood. He said, *"You know, Jerome, I've made seventeen million dollars this year. Not all of it is mine. Maybe only six or eight million of it is mine. But usually it takes me all year to make that much. It's been a pretty good year."*

It was only the 20th of January. He made this money while at the same time taking the same ten-day class I was taking. How do you respond to that? I was blown away by that but I was cool about it. I figured I'd better shut up and listen.

He said, *"There are two kinds of people in this class. There are the 'for world peace' people. They're humanitarians and they spend half of their time making the 'money people' wrong. Then there are the 'how to get rich' people. They're the money people. You look, act, and talk like a money person but I believe you're a closet humanitarian. "*

He looked at me skeptically giving me the side eye. It seemed kind of funny to me. I almost felt like apologizing for being a reasonably decent guy. I smiled. He had hit a chord in me. I didn't want him to stop talking though.

I said, *"I am a closet humanitarian. I grew up with 15 people. We had to share everything. I don't mind helping people. I just don't want to go broke doing it. "* It was the truth. That seemed to make enough sense for him to reconcile his concerns.

He continued. He said, *"People think it's about money but money is not it. It's just a way to keep score."*

Now he's really got my attention. I had always thought it was how much you make. He went on, *"Money is a medium of exchange and the reason most people don't make much money is because they don't know what they have to exchange. They don't know why people pay them.*

Another reason they don't make much money is because what they have to exchange doesn't have a lot of value. A lot of people can type a letter or flip a burger. Hell, you can hire a doctor or a lawyer today, fire him today, and get another one today. With all of their skills, hospitals and HMO's push doctors around all the time. And they screw up a lot of the good investments too. A lot of them are good doctors but lousy investors with a lot of money. You have to do your due diligence. They usually pay too much and drive up prices.

Another reason people don't make much money is because they don't know how to duplicate (enhance, maximize, leverage) what they have to exchange."

And then he said something that etched into my brain like an engraver. He said, *"But wealth is the ability to survive a number of days forward without the addition of more work and without a drop in your lifestyle. At that point the question becomes, 'How many days forward can you survive if you stop working today?' That is your level of wealth. You have doctors making two or three hundred thousand dollars a year but if they don't go to work on Monday, they lose the house, the boat, the car, you name it. Wealthy people work once and get paid over and over again. Wealth is it."*

I knew he had given me a big key to wealth. I got it in my head. Now I have to find the door that the key opens. I said, *"How can I do that?"*

He seemed a little annoyed with the question. He said, *"Think! Think!"*

I thought about our conversation for months. How can I work once and get paid over and over again. The more I thought about it, the more answers came to me. I could create a specialized mailing list once and sell it many times. I could join a network marketing company, build a big down line once, and get paid over and over again. I could write a book once and sell it a million times. I could make a CD once (*Jerome and the Boys Rap On*) and every time it's played on the radio I get paid. I could invent something once, manufacture it or lease the rights to use it, I could buy a multi-unit apartment building once. My grandkids could live there twenty years from now and I would still be getting paid on it.

*****

Now fast forward to November and December of 1994. I had been invited to Australia and New Zealand to present a seminar on the system I created on how to hire and train under-privileged urban youth normally ages 17 to 21. I was teaching them how to run my business and they were doing a phenomenal job.

I was staying with a nice lady, about 55 years old. Her looks were average. She was articulate, but not eloquent. She had a high school education, and six kids who were grown and gone. But she lived in the unquestionably best part of town in a big city. There were mansions with tennis courts, great townhouses, outdoor cafes, and beautiful people all around us. It was a really nice place to be. She told me that in 1981-82 she had a network marketing business with six kids in tow. After two years her husband said he wanted her to stay home. He wanted his dinner on the table and for her to stop dragging his kids all over the place. So she stopped actively working the business and simply managed her business after that. Her husband left her a few years later. Yet her organization continued to grow. He made his move too soon, but that's another story.

When I first got there, she got a check for almost $4000-American. The Australian dollar was worth 56 cents of the American dollar so the check was worth over $7000 -Australian. It was no big deal to me. I had four retail shops. It's Christmas time. Retailers live for Christmas time, and I was making money hand over fist, way more money than that. I had a bankroll. One month later, before I left, she got another check for almost $5000 - American. Again, it was no big deal to me. I had four retail shops. It's Christmas time.

Then one day she came into the living room where I was sitting on the carpet. She said, *"As of today, the seminar is in the black. We're in profit now. How would you like your wife to come over for a week, shop, swim, and sightsee?"*

I just looked at her without saying a word. Understand, in the American Midwest it's winter. It's freezing outside with ice and snow everywhere. But in Australia, on the other side of the equator in the southern hemisphere, it's summer time with temperatures in the 80's every day. People are at the beach every day letting it all hang out. What man on the globe wouldn't want to call his wife and tell her to go to the airport, pick up a round trip ticket to fly to the other side of the world to shop, swim, and sightsee for a week? What woman wouldn't give her man big brownie points and a gold star for doing that? Every man wants his woman to look at him all googlie-eyed and think, *"That's my man!"* with a great big smile on her face. That's what we work for. But it's Christmas time. I'm not about to yank my wife out of those retail shops. It wouldn't make sense. It was totally out of the question.

That's when Bill popped into my head, *"Wealth is the ability to survive a number of days forward without the addition of more work and without a drop in your lifestyle. How many days forward can you survive if you stop working today? That is your level of wealth. Wealthy people work once and get paid over and over again. Wealth is it."*

In that moment, I realized I had been working my whole life for money and security instead of real wealth and real freedom. I realized the lady I was staying with had real wealth and I only had money. I didn't even have security. She had freedom. She was far better off than I. This time I got it in my heart.

It hurt me that I could not call my wife with the invitation. I made a promise to myself right then to never again work for money and security, to only work for real wealth and real freedom. My rules had changed. I had to start from scratch. I had to re-construct the way I live. Ultimately I have come to believe that my relationships with God, my family, and friends are my greatest form of wealth. The journey continues. I'm still a work in progress but that's another story. Thankfully, I have no idea what I'm in for.

Book Six

Forgiveness

Forgiveness opened a door and released me to receive my good.

Miracles

A miracle is an extraordinary event that happens to ordinary people.

To recover from a serious illness or accident is a miracle. To experience love or forgiveness is a miracle. To be able to drive down the road and pass hundreds of cars on the opposite side daily and not one of them comes into your lane ever, that is a miracle. The birth of a child happens every day but is such a miracle that when it happens to us we remember that date for the rest of our lives. Miracles happen all of the time to everyone and they come in all sizes. When unrecognized we think of them as commonplace like driving down the road. Only when something goes awry do we realize how much we took for granted. When recognized we marvel at how fortunate we are. A miracle is not luck. Luck is preparation plus opportunity. They look similar but you can prepare or even expect to be lucky with hard work, persistence and good intent. A miracle doesn't require any of that. They just come.

A miracle is a gift. It is the grace of God smiling on you. You cannot work for it. You don't deserve it. It's a gift. However, you can leave room for miracles by putting yourself in a position where a miracle can happen. How? When you give more than you have to, you normally receive more than you expect.

*****

My father was a man who liked you or didn't like you. I don't know why, but he didn't like me. And after a while it went both ways. I got fed up with trying to be pleasing to him. We never got along. We loved each other but we didn't like each other at all. It was not an issue for us. This presented some anguish for my mother, but not for him and me. We were clear about it, locked and loaded and pointing at each other. That's where we were. I finally told him when I was ten or 11, "*I don't like you. You don't like me.*

Why don't we just leave each other alone?" and I meant that. From that day, I never asked him for anything, not a hamburger, a pair of sox, nothing. I never once spoke a disrespectful word to my father, but with a glance I could deliver the same callous disregard for his feelings as he treated mine.

I'm sure that he would have helped me as much as he could if I would come to him and asked because he was a dutiful person. But I flat out refused to ask and he flat out refused to offer. I came home one day with the sole of my sneakers flapping. It was before high school time. We looked at each other. We understood each other perfectly. I was thinking, *"I'm your son. You know I need some shoes. Buy me some."*

He was thinking, *"I'm your father. I know you need some shoes. I'll buy you some. Ask me."* Then both of us put this *'Up yours'* look on our faces and we parted. Not a word need be spoken. We understood. He would think, *"You'll need me before I need you."*

I would think, *"I'm going to figure out a way to not need you."* We meant the other no harm. We offered the other no sway. And so it went for decades.

In an off-handed way, I have to give my father credit for who I developed into. When a person is under pressure usually one of three things will come forth. First, some will crumble. Second, some will express their criminal nature. Third, some get very creative. I am the latter. Even now, I can think of five ways to get one thing done. I started my first business at age seventeen. Not because of my business acumen but because I wanted things. Asking was out of the question. I had no desire to dodge the police. So I figured out a legal way to get them. I've had businesses ever since. Again, I have to give credit to my father. Years later I realized how much we are alike. Although I'm genuinely warm and friendly, I still have to ever be on guard for what I call *'the asshole within.'* Thankfully I got compassion from my mother. I choose to be gracious.

My father could swear with a flair unknown to mankind. He was great at it. His sentence structure, cadence, diction and rhythm were impeccable. He could free style curse you out. The unusual combinations and strings of profanities he could hurl at a moments' notice was pure art form.

My father loved animals and children. He was at ease with them. He was protective of his family, including me. He could mess with us but nobody else could. He lived on his principles. He got to the bottom line quickly. He went to work every day. I always respected that. He was loyal to his friends and they were loyal to him. He wasn't a bad guy. He just wasn't my guy.

He had a great, caustic sense of humor. He didn't really tell jokes but he was a master of the wise crack, the smart remark, and the quick retort. His humor had a sharp point, usually with some unsuspecting victim dangling on the other end. If you could take the hit, he was hilarious. If you could dish it back so much the better. If you had tender feelings you'd better have a handkerchief at the ready. I resist the urge to be like that. I've learned to bite my tongue.

I left home the first time when I was fifteen, then for good at eighteen. Later I moved no closer than six hundred miles away for the next twenty years. I would visit for a day or two, every four or five years. That was more than enough for me.

In the late eighties, my father got very ill so I came back to make sure everything was taken care of. I am a dutiful person as well. I also knew he would need me before I needed him. He knew it too. But I wanted to be a good son and my parents seemed to appreciate it. My relationship with my father got better. It was more like two guys sitting at a poker table with pistols on the table but not pointed at each other. It was better.

I got married in 1990 and moved again, this time only ninety miles away to Milwaukee. We would visit almost every Sunday. My wife and my mother loved being together. They could talk for hours. They would just disappear to see a movie, get an ice cream cone, or even a cocktail. My mother never did that with anyone but her. I also liked the small dose way it went all the way around.

In 1996 my father got very sick again and was in the hospital for two months. My wife and I owned retail units in shopping malls. The malls opened at 9:00 a.m. and closed at 9:00 p.m. I would drive that ninety miles every night after closing to see my father. I wanted him and the staff to know that somebody was looking out. I had his back. After all, I could mess with him but nobody else could. I would spend the night and leave when the shift changed and the sun came up. I often wondered, *"Is this love or is this duty?"* In either case I was holding up my end. After a month or so, he could walk or talk no longer.

One night, in the middle of the night while I was sleeping in the chair next to his bed, he reached over and grabbed my hand. His grasp was surprisingly firm. I stood up and still holding hands we really looked at each other for a long time.

It was love. It was clean. It was pure. It was radiant love. In that moment a thirty year mutual standoff was erased. Our burden was lifted. All debt was forgiven. We got a reprieve. Before that moment, I could not have imagined or even hoped for such peace and accord between us. It was a gift that keeps giving. It was the grace of God smiling on us. It was a miracle.

My father was laid to rest three weeks later. Yet we both rest in peace with each other.

*****

The back story...

My grandfather died when my father was about ten years old. From that point on, he was the man of his family. He had several younger siblings and a mom to look out for from where he stood. He was driving a bootleg liquor truck during the depression and prohibition by the time he was 12 years old.

His mother got a job in a Catholic parish where they didn't pay much, but her children were able to get a great education for free. He too was able to go to high school there. To others, it was a big deal because then as now, people had to pay to go to Catholic school. This was during the great depression. To this very day, my father's side of the family remain Catholic.

He didn't talk about it much but growing up was tough for him and high school was incredibly hard. He was one of a very few Black kids, including his siblings, in the whole parish, much less in the school. In his senior year he was harassed, roughed up, 'put in his place,' and chased home along the railroad tracks every day for weeks by three White boys. It was the late 1930's. By then Eastern Europe was already under attack. Western Europe was starting to be threatened by the German war machine. One day on his way to school he picked up a tennis ball sized rock and put it in his pocket. This day when they surrounded him on the tracks, he busted one of them in the head with the rock. He went down. The other two ran. He threw the rock and hit the second one in the head. He went down. The third one ran back into the church. My father ran in after him and gave him a beat down right in front of the alter. He was given a choice. Go to prison or go to the army. In 1938 he began serving his country.

He was married in 1940. They had a child in early 1941. His honorable discharged was to be completed in January of 1942, but Pearl Harbor was bombed December 7th 1941. WWII was on and he was not released for another four years. The greatest generation returned home in 1945 and life resumed in this new American normal.

He probably took on too much responsibility as a child. I know he had been bullied. He probably saw way too much racism, poverty, misery, and death as a young man. He probably didn't have a working concept of what a good husband or father was. Damaged people damage other people. I didn't know all of that as a child. All I knew was that I caught a lot of unwarranted mistreatment that I didn't have coming. His gripe was not with me.

133

It felt like he was condescending, dismissive, or trying to crush my spirit. I'm number five of six boys growing up so I already knew versions of those feelings and that behavior. I can take it on the chin if I'm wrong. But I don't like catching crap for nothing. I don't shake up easily. I'm not a good victim. We got along sometimes. We never said it but we really did love each other and had some traits in common. I can see his face in mine. We just didn't like each other. So I mostly stayed out of his way.

I also have endured hardships as a child and as an adult because of my refusal to be diminished by or ask him for anything. I could also see the difference in how he treated me and my other siblings. I bought my own clothes, cars, and paid my own way through college. Those times have become character-building exclamation points in my life. I value them now. Part of the joy of parenting is having the ability and willingness to sacrifice and accommodate some of the wants and needs of your children. Several years after he died it occurred to me how tough it must have been for him as a parent to have a child who showed the matching level of tolerance, intolerance, acceptance, rejection, and/or contempt for him as he expressed for the child. What must it be like for him to have a child who would rather do without food, clothing, or shelter than come to him for anything. I'm sure at some point he had to look in the mirror and ask, "how did it come to this?"

I'm grateful that we were able to heal things between us in the nick of time. It is a huge blessing. The sting is gone. I certainly recommend that everyone make the effort to clear things up with family and friends if they can. As an adult, I do set boundaries while making a conscience effort to pay attention, encourage, show affection, listen, and treat children with the kindness and respect I always valued. Thank God for his tender mercies, and his miracles.

I Don't Have Anything for You

He asked if he could stay at my house.

Our family has been on this block since the 1920'S. I never actually thought of this as my house anyway. It's our family house. It's home for a lot of people. Generations of us come here or even lived here over the years. This is the place where relative's kids run away from home and come to my house. If somebody's wife puts them out, they might come to my house. If someone wants to move back in town, they may come here first. I had a 17 year old cousin who got drunk and didn't want to go home to face the music so he came to my house at 2:00 a.m. I called his mother to let her know he's okay. He stayed the night. I chewed him out in the morning and fed him a good breakfast.

So with my nephew I thought, '*Why not. He's my nephew. He's been coming here since he was one week old. He's always welcome here.*' This is where he and his brother spent countless weekends and whole summers. My request of him was simple: "*Clean something; cook something; repair something; or pay for something.*" I figured that was very reasonable. After all, he's a grown man now about 40 years old with a wife and two small children.

I told him that his wife and family were welcome to stay here too. I was okay with that. I had only met her once but this is home for all of us. His wife and kids chose to stay with her family 150 miles away. That was fine. I figured we'd see them from time to time. I helped him get a job where I had some influence. I treated him like family as I should. He would go to visit his family on the weekends but they never came here. This went on for a year and a half.

He went to work every day and was pleasant to be around but he never picked up a bill, never mopped a floor, cut a blade of grass, washed a window, or even washed a dish that he didn't use. He only cooked for himself. Maybe in his mind he was trying to stay out to the way. But to us it was him not making any impact at all or adding any value to our home experience. This bothered me a lot but I was advised by other family members who love both of us not to make a big deal out of it. So I didn't. No harm, no foul.

One year I got laid off of my job right before Christmas. Although I had a tiny business selling garments it wasn't enough to cover the bills. I missed my January and February house payments. I was late on my March payment but not 30 days late. The mortgage company sent me a Foreclosure Notice about 75-80 days into this ordeal. I told my nephew about it that evening when he got home.

He said, *"So what are you going to do about it?"* like he was a bystander.

I just looked at him. This is the one I thought of as the 'heir apparent,' the one who would become a leader in our family and community over time. He's the one who understood me. He's the one who would jump in a foxhole with me. Then I thought, *"Maybe he's just not quick in the moment. Maybe it didn't register."*

But every day he would come home and ask me what I'm doing about the house, how's it going, and things like that. Not once did he ask what he could do or offer to help in any way. He didn't say, *"I don't have much money but you can keep this check (from the job I got him). Or let me look through my contacts to see if there may be someone who could help."* He didn't offer to sit down and strategize with me. Not once did he lift a finger or make even the smallest gesture to support.

He went to see his family on the weekend as usual. When he got back he inquired about the status of the house again. That's when I called him out.

"Do you have any ideas? I don't want to lose 'our' home."

This was his reply exactly verbatim. *"I don't have any money. I'm not going to sell any garments. I don't have anything for you."*

That summed it up precisely. Perhaps I shouldn't have been surprised. He had been showing me that for over a year. But it became crystal clear in that moment. At that point there was nothing else to talk about. As far as I was concerned he had thrown me to the lions. He had betrayed me personally, our home, and our family. He had committed treason and jumped ship on all of us. Whatever relationship we had was dead to me.

I said, *"I might get shot down. But I'm not going to lie down. And I'm not going to get dragged down by dead weight. You can visit but this is not your home anymore. Get your shit and get out right now."*

He said, *"Where am I going to go?"*

"Go to a shelter. Find a bridge to stay under. Sleep in your car. Make a friend. I don't care where you go just like you don't care where I go. Get out right now."

It took me almost two years to save the house with the grace of God. I would think about him every now and then but he was simply not a part of my life anymore. It wasn't a simmering or angry view of him. I had no ill will towards him at all. In fact I wish him well. I wasn't avoiding contact with him. When I thought about it, I'm not sure that he even understood the magnitude of what he had done or not done, and how it affected me. I just felt no need to ever see or hear from him again, ever, period. It wasn't a mean place in my heart for him. It was a cold place.

Seven years later I was talking to a very good friend. Our conversations are generally wide ranging. I respect his opinion. We were talking about our goals and how to manifest them. I asked him to look up a scripture passage I had heard in church that Sunday (Mark 11:22-24). It talks about how to get what you want. But when I went back to check it for myself I read the next two verses as well (Mark 11:25-26). They say how you must forgive people 'first' before you get what you want.

He and I talked a few days later. Among other things we exchanged stories about our troubled relationships with our fathers. I told him that in the end, my father and I had healed our relationship. There was no more hostility there for me. Then he asked me a profound question.

He said, *"Have you forgiven your father?"*

He had also read those two additional verses. This happened on a Friday. I had never thought about it like that. It brought to mind another verse I had read (Romans 13:8) saying, *"Owe no man anything but to love one another."* I knew my father and I had a moment when love showed through and the electric charge of anger was gone from us. It was a moment of peace and accord. We laid our weapons down. I don't know if it was a moment of forgiveness though. I thought it was done. But now I had to ask myself if I actually forgave my father for his offenses against me. When I examined myself, the answer was yes I had forgiven him.

Then I asked myself if there was anyone else I may need to forgive? My nephew's face popped up immediately. For the next several days I thought about my nephew quite a bit. On a Tuesday morning for the first time in seven years, I called my nephew.

I asked him to hear me out. He did. I explained everything I said above and more. I told him how painful it was not only to be thrown to the lions, but also after receiving every possible kindness from me for a year and a half, it was him that didn't lift a finger to help. When I needed support, his response was literally, *"I don't have anything for you."* He just let it happen. And worst of all, after all of that time staying at my home with me, our home, he never once brought his family around to this place where we've been for generations. If I saw his children playing in the front yard right now, I wouldn't even know who they were. The things he cared about the most, his family, he kept far away from me and the rest of our family. The 150 mile distance was more like the other side of the world. None of us who had embraced him his whole life had seen him or his family in years. I told him that it was probably as hard for him to hear all of this as it was for me to say. He confirmed that.

Then I told him the reason I called was not to beat him up but rather to tell him this, "*I forgive you. And I love you.*"

You Saved Her

"I like you. Do you like me? Put the answer in the box." She handed me the note right before I went home for lunch. We were a bunch of little kids with no front teeth in first grade. She was a nice girl. I didn't want to hurt her feelings. I liked her okay but not anything more than that. I'm six years old. It's first grade.

Aunt Marion was always home for us at lunch time. She was a cook at a very fine restaurant so she worked evenings and nights. She was my mother's older sister. She had never married or had children, and still lived in my grandfather's house, as we all did. There were my siblings and two other sets of cousins in the house, five or six boys and three girls. She loved all of us but the girls were like her little dolls. She would put Vaseline on them so they wouldn't be ashy, and then dress them up in frilly dresses, white gloves and sox with lace, beautiful little coats, and Patton leather shoes. Those girls shined like new money.

I overheard my mother tell her, *"You shouldn't be buying all of these expensive clothes for them. It's too much."*

Aunt Marion said, *"I know I get nice things for the girls. And they don't necessarily need the things I buy. But please don't take away the joy I get from giving."* Those words still ring in my ears today and have become more meaningful over time.

She would teach them etiquette, how to make hor d'oeuvres and little sandwiches with the crust cut off. We boys would plot on how to get some of that grub. She would take them out for brunch or 'high tea.'

She was a sweet woman, sensitive, with a desire to please others though she always seemed kind of weak and unsure of herself, not wanting to impose, and a little helpless. Even as a child I could tell we all wanted to protect her. You could hurt her feelings so nobody ever fussed at her.

I got home feeling perplexed about this note. I wasn't going to tell the other kids in the house. I knew they would laugh and make fun of me. So I went to Aunt Marion. I asked her to promise me not to tell anyone, ever. She agreed. Then I read her the note. The answer was simple. *"Just tell her you like her as a friend."* She helped me write the reply.

Later that evening my mother, other aunts, and grandmother were all hugging and kissing me, telling me how cute I was with my little note. Everybody knew. Everybody in the house knew. I was totally embarrassed. The kids laughed and poked fun at me asking me who my girlfriend was. I felt my trust had been 100% betrayed. Even though I loved her, and I know she meant no harm, my trust for her was gone. I kept Aunt Marion at arm's length emotionally for the next twenty years.

*****

It was warm outside, a beautiful night. God had sprinkled extra stars in the sky. I was standing at a pay phone 1200 miles away in the middle of nowhere when I called her.

"Aunt Marion, this is your nephew. I just wanted you to know I really love you."

There was long pause before she said, *"I love you too."* as she started to cry on the phone. It was like a big yolk had been lifted off of my neck, maybe hers too.

Another nine years passed before I moved back to my home town. Aunt Marion had had a stroke and was in a nursing home by then. She was surprised and happy to see me when I walked in. After a little small talk I said, *"Get up. Take a walk with me."*

"I can't."

"Yes you can. Get up."

"I can't walk."

"Come on auntie. Just walk the bathroom door. It's right there across the room ten steps away. You can do it. Come on."

I know it was a challenge for her but she did it. I came back every day or two. Each time we'd go a little bit further, to the door, across the hall, to the picture in the hall, to the fire extinguisher, to the next door. Her balance improved, her stride became more steady. She stood up a little straighter. I could see her getting stronger. I could see defeat losing its grip. She was pleased with herself.

You know how nursing homes have that 'old people smell?' There is usually a big room with a TV and lots of windows where they congregate, some walking, others in wheel chairs, all in varying degrees of physical and mental health. Some get visitors. Many don't. And here's Aunt Marion, an invalid, weak and not walking, who gets a young good looking visitor every day or two. I could see them chatter after a while when they saw us together. She was walking now and in good spirits. In less than two months she could walk all the way down the hall. She could get to the elevator and even make it to the patio where she would sit in the sun, close her eyes, and let it shine on her face. We would only stay out there 15 or 20 minutes. We didn't really talk much but she was happy. I could tell. It was good for both of us.

Then I got a job. I just couldn't come anymore. She was dead the next month. In my head I know I didn't kill her but in my heart it sure felt like I did. I felt horrible about it. I carried that with me for years.

Twenty plus years later I had a new girlfriend. Her father and his siblings had just put her grandmother in a nursing home. We were talking in the car late one night parked across the street from the building where her grandmother was. She was talking about the ups and downs of her grandmother's life and the possibility of taking her out of there. And I told her this very story about Aunt Marion. I will be forever thankful for what she told me next.

She said, "*You didn't kill her. You saved her. You didn't let her down. You lifted her up. You validated her and showed her what love really means. You gave her an incredible gift. You brought her joy.*"

Again a yoke was lifted off of my neck. She showed me I had not abandoned Aunt Marion. I had been paying a debt I didn't owe. I could forgive myself. Praise God. That's what I carry now.

Book Seven

Freedom

Freedom and wisdom come at no small expense. They are rare, elusive, and take time to acquire. That's why they're so valuable.

Freedom – Wisdom

Freedom is not free. The price of freedom is you must be willing to be your own master. (unknown).

You must be willing to think for yourself, rise or fall on the strength of your conviction, and accept your own judgment. You must be okay with no one instructing you or telling you what to do. You must be willing to be wrong, to look like a fool, to get knocked down and then get up, to be persecuted. Everyone won't like you. Some may try to discredit you or claim your ideas as their own. You must become comfortable with uncertainty and be willing to look in the mirror and confront yourself. You may face disaster. Be willing to make mistakes. They do come. You can spare yourself a degree of aggravation by learning from other people's mistakes. Sometimes you must forgive others and yourself. Give the benefit of the doubt. We all need it sometimes. Be it large or small, freedom demands that you must defend it, occupy the space it grants you, and demonstrate why you should possess it.

You must be willing to stand alone, to set your own standards, to challenge the status quo, speak truth to power, to help others, to serve, to give more than you take. Be patient and listen actively even to braggarts, the boring, and fools. Even they may drop a pearl of wisdom sometimes. Be willing to win and win big. Accept that as you demonstrate people may want to follow you whether you wanted to be a leader or not. You are responsible for how and where you lead others. Be willing to accept the mantle of leadership. You will have to wear many hats. It's not a straight or easy road. But once you taste freedom it's hard to go back.

The price of wisdom is experience + reflection, and when possible, correction.

We all have experiences every day. But through reflection is where you can derive deeper meaning and draw lessons when needed. Without reflection you can easily repeat mistakes, miss opportunities, or just stay where you are instead of learning and moving forward. Both freedom and wisdom come at no small expense. They are rare, elusive, and take time to acquire. That's why they're so valuable.

Genghis

When I was seventeen years old I took a three-day class called Mind Dynamics. It was held at McCormick Place, a large convention center in Chicago. There were over 100 people in the class and I was definitely the youngest one in there. It cost a few hundred dollars which was huge for me at the time. We did a lot of different exercises and read a book (Think and Grow Rich).

On the third day the originator of the course, a man in his early fifties, came to speak. He was a mega-millionaire and he brought with him an eagle, a real live eagle named Genghis. The bird sat on a very sturdy log perch about four feet tall and he had a hood on to cover his eyes. He had to wear a hood because apparently eagles are high strung birds and they get nervous. You don't really want a high strung bird with three-inch talons and a beak that can rip open a carcass to get nervous in a room full of people at a convention center.

Then the speaker began to tell his story. He had had many different jobs and professions. He had been a teacher and later owned several businesses. It really didn't matter what he did, only that everything he ever did failed.

So three and a half years earlier, he was on his way home from yet again another failure. It was the middle of the night during a tremendous thunder storm as he was driving down the highway feeling sorry for himself. Literally, a bolt of lightning struck in the distance behind the car and it lit up the car. In that moment he looked into the rear view mirror into his own eyes and for the first time he saw himself.

For the first time in his life he thought, *"Maybe it's me. Maybe I'm the cause of my own failures."* Before that he had always blamed the economy, the product, the circumstances, his business associates, and anybody but himself. So he made some major decisions that changed everything in his life such as:

147

First, I will take full responsibility for everything that happens in my life, period. If I'm not responsible, who is? I want to be on top of the circumstances, not under them. Second, Nothing is worth the price of me worrying about it. If I can do something about it, I will. If not, I will not worry." At this time he was $90,000 in debt. He said, *"I'll let them worry."*

In short, he made several life changing decisions.

Then he started to talk about sparrows. They're little birds. So during inclement weather they will fly down to the lower branches of trees, into the bushes, on to the ground, under cars, behind barriers or anywhere they can go to escape the wrath of the storm; whereas an eagle will fly into the clouds and rise above the storm.

Then he carefully took the hood off of this bird and said, *"Fly Genghis!"*

And this bird took off, 'whoosh-whoosh' flapping those huge wings. He only took about four or five strokes and Genghis soared around that room eight feet above our heads with his 4-5 foot wing span fully extended. He landed back on his perch, and then flexed his shoulders and talons so we could not mistake his capacity to take care of business. He turned his head both ways so we could marvel at his powerful beak, and then stared at us with those piercing eyes to let us know that he was watching us too. He was magnificent. He was magnificent!

The speaker gently put the hood back on Genghis then looked into the audience at each one of us and said, *"You must throw off the shackles of fear and ignorance that bind your wings and rise above the storm. Be an eagle in life!"*

I knew he was speaking directly to me. I made a decision that day that has guided the rest of my life.

Now I'm speaking directly to you.

Student Task Force

I am an alumni of a Historically Black College/University (HBCU). Several years ago I, along with about 50 other very professional, educated, well-meaning people were invited to a HBCU for a three-day event. I went for three years in a row. The intent was to motivate, enlighten, and assist students to be ready for the world of work after graduation. These were all people to be admired, not only for their accomplishments, but also for how far they had come from to get to where they are. Many of them were the first in their families to go to college. Several were from small southern towns and remember picking cotton and growing their own food. Some were from places where the only Black folks who wore suit and ties or dresses to work were preachers and teachers. That's it. I'm from a northern city but I'm only the second person in my whole extended family to graduate from college. All of these people were well respected in their communities and rightfully so. Being invited into this group was like a personal acknowledgement and point of pride for many. I felt honored to be included with them. We were split into small teams of three to four people and would go talk to classrooms most of each day.

On the first day we answered a questionnaire, at our discretion, about the kind of work we did, approximate income range, possible career paths, and job satisfaction. I was surprised to find that I was making double or even triple the money that most of them were making. What stuck out most over time was the 'job satisfaction' assessment. Most of them stated on paper that they like their jobs, were good at them, or comfortable in their positions. Although quietly in casual conversation, several of them would tell me what they were doing on the side, or express their desire to work for themselves.

Some people worked for the government. A few were military officers. They really did look impressive in their spit shined shoes and crisp uniforms with all the bars, badges, and medals. Others worked for city, county, state, and federal. They talked about their agencies and departments, services they provided, and how to qualify and apply for those kinds of jobs. Others were non-profit or corporate executives and management people. They talked about a broad range of topics including: interviews, salary, how to dress, office politics, red flags, perks, and advantages of all kinds. We all talked about the value of a good education. All of them were really solid people and totally supportive of the students. I learned a lot from them as well. I had big respect for them and their hard-earned gains.

When it was my turn to speak I would ask the students:

Q. How many of you would like a really great job? Raise your hands.

A. Everybody.

Q. How many of you would like to be rich, travel around the world, get wealthy, be free, and then maybe create a way to double it?

A. Everybody.

Q. How many of you know someone who has a great job and is rich?

A. Nobody.

Then I would talk to them about owning their own businesses. I talked about investing, leverage, and creating a legacy for their families and their future. I talked about freedom. I told them that as much as I valued my education and wouldn't trade it for anything, how I make my money had absolutely nothing to do with what my major was. I told them that jobs are not everywhere but opportunity is. It had to do with helping people to solve problems, creating solutions, and gaining new perspectives to issues. I told them it's not just about what you do. It's about who you are. I let them know I have had jobs but only as a short term solution for a cash flow problem or for what I could learn.

One of the first things people ask, even to a perfect stranger is, *"What do you do?"* I guess it's a legitimate question from a pigeon-hole, boxy, contextual point of view but it simply misses the point. Everyone has many facets of their lives. What do they care about? I am not what I do. I am who I am and I do many things. It is extremely common for people to change what they do yet fundamentally remain the same person. All of us are precious and have something special to contribute. I don't want to just *'get in where I fit in.'* This is my life. I can't predict everything to come but I can design my life trajectory. We have a choice.

I told them that in America, most people think they must: 'do' something so they can 'have' something so they can 'be' something. I always think about 'being something' and then 'doing something,' so I can 'have something.' My beingness (who I am) dictates my doingness and havingness.

I never want to work just to earn a living. I never want to compromise the integrity of my dreams just so I can pay bills. Don't discount your dreams. They are a powerful expression of who you are. I don't want to prostitute myself for money going to a job I don't like and toughing it out for however many years. I want to express my own natural gifts, talents, and experiences to improve life on the planet. I want to leave an inheritance for my children's children. I want to create artifacts that change the way people live. I want to give away an increasingly significant portion of my earnings and never even feel it. I work for real wealth, real freedom, and real happiness, not just for money and security. That way I can be true to who I am and live without regret.

I let them know I'm not judging other people. I am speaking for myself. By all means I respect anyone who will do an honest days' work for an honest days' pay. I absolutely respect anyone who does what they have to do to take care of themselves, their families, put food on the table, and contribute to society. Still my heart goes out to those who work way too hard for way too little as well as those who earn a good income but hate their jobs. I come from a multi-generational family of people who get up and go to work every day. I enjoy the sense of accomplishment in a hard

151

day's work. It's the feeling of drudgery and toil that I wouldn't wish on anyone.

I like to think that I added substantial value to the experience for everyone concerned. I like to think that I may have touched some student's lives with a different perspective that while they're looking for a job, to keep an eye open for opportunity. But maybe my opinions were too far outside of the mainstream. Maybe, unintentionally, I offended some folks. After the third year I was not invited back anymore. For the student's sake, I wish I had been.

Nonetheless, Historically Black Colleges and Universities are still the only places in America where young Black students are 100% expected to assume a higher vision of themselves. They can go there, be validated and totally recognized for their accomplishments. They can interact with scholars and role models who look like them, and be surrounded by hundreds or thousands of other young Black people who are challenging themselves and doing very positive things every day. I enthusiastically celebrate that.

More Than a Dollar

On a bitterly cold January evening just about sundown there she was with a four year old child, a toddler, and one in a stroller. She was a pitiful looking soul swatting at one's hand, hushing another, and rolling the stroller back and forth to keep the baby quiet.

The shopping mall stretched over three square city blocks. The bulk of it actually cut off one street and had a walkway overpass that straddled the second street on the upper level. The overpass was full of brightly colored pushcarts, art, and an interesting awry of oddities and knickknacks. It was a festive well-lit place. Even though the windows were floor to ceiling, they were really part of the decor. From the inside it was easy to ignore the cold winter days. At night, they reflected everything back to the inside. From the outside it looked like all was warm and well for any who entered the overpass.

Below, cars and delivery trucks breezed through oblivious to anything except for what was straight ahead. On both sides of the street were entrances to the mall to accommodate foot traffic. There was an outer door by the sidewalk and an inner door about eight feet in that opened into the shopping areas. The double doors kept the cold and wind from blowing directly in. I should have crossed up top because I didn't have a coat on. But I did have on a sweater. Besides, even in the cold, forty yards is a manageable dash. On the other side, between those two doors is where she stood.

"Sir, can you spare a few dollars so I can feed my kids?"

I looked at her for a long moment. I guess she sized me up when she saw me coming across, and decided she might be able to get a 'few' dollars out of me instead of the usual 'one or two.' It kind of ticked me off because I felt like I was getting played. It felt like the kids were being used as compelling props. They just looked up at you, as cute as a button. They were innocent. Who could say no to that? I just happened to be the next 'Venus Fly

Trap' sucker who floated across this sorry scene. I wasn't a real person to her. I was just some guy who represented cash in her pocket. I knew it and she knew I knew it. The same way women can tell what's on a man's mind when he keeps looking further down instead of looking them in the face.

I had a shop in that mall so I dressed appropriately every day. And every day someone would try to hit me up for something, usually cash. I don't look down my nose at people because I've been down and out on more than one occasion myself. Respect to them but as a matter of fact, there are several kinds of people with their hand out on a regular basis. Some have handicaps. Others with a temporary situation who promise to pay you back the next time they see you. Money for food was a common request. Evangelist doing their praise thing with a cup in their hand was another.

There was one guy who actually told me, "*Everybody needs somebody to give something to.*" like he was supposed to be my own private charity case.

One guy would tell you straight out, "*I need a drink.*" He would say, "*Now reflect brother…*" and then tell you a fantastic sad story. Then he would forget that he had talked to me a few weeks earlier, and would give me a whole different sad story the next time. Although I'd usually say no, I must admit, that guy was phenomenal. He was the king of the panhandlers to me. Out of respect for his craft, sometimes I had to 'toss him a bone' because of the entertainment value.

The bottom line is, for some of these people, this is their job. It's what they do. I'm as cool as the next guy but I didn't want to get handled or have the same people pecking at me every day.

I was on the way to get my shoes shined. My mother always said she could tell a lot about a man by how he took care of his shoes. I'm not exactly sure what she meant by that, but I didn't want to be on the wrong side of it. Anyway, I crossed the street and there she was. It wasn't like I didn't have a few dollars to spare but

I worked hard for my money. I had to examine myself for a moment. *'Am I just a heartless, greedy man with no compassion for a needy mother with hungry children?'* I don't think so. I make a serious effort to give more than I take. I'm always wary though, of responding to requests of 'something for nothing' no matter where it comes from. I trusted my instincts. It felt like emotional blackmail with the little kids' right there. I knew that feeling from way back and I didn't like it. It grated at my core. If she wanted some cash from me, she had to earn it.

I said, "*Is this what you want your kids to see? Is this what you want them to learn from you? They don't listen to what you say. They look at who you are and what you do. We were poor too but none of us knew it. I don't know what you've been through or how you got here, but having your kids in this cold place watching you ask strangers for money doesn't cut it.*"

I heard myself talking, right in front of the kids no less. As valid as it may have been it still sounded ugly, even to me. I realized she was having a hard enough time without me on her case sitting in judgment. That doesn't cut it either. I didn't even mind helping the lady and especially the kids. I just didn't want to feel like a walking dollar bill. Nor did I want to kick her when she was down. How could we extract some dignity out of this for both of us?

I told her, "*If you can tell me how to make a dollar worth more than a dollar, I'll give you ten dollars. If you can't, I'll give you nothing. I'm making a fifteen minute run. Have the answer when I get back.*"

It was hard but it was fair. When I returned, I asked the question, "*How can you make a dollar worth more than a dollar?*"

She said, "*I could go to the flower man and get 12 roses for $7.00 and sell them for $1.00 each. I could go to Sam's Club and buy a box of M&M's and sell them for a profit.*"

She looked at me with anticipation, not for the money but for approval like a kid who answered a question on a test. I smiled, then reached into my pocket and gave her the $10.00 I had promised for completing the task, and another $3.00 as a bonus for the 'few dollars' she had asked for in the beginning.

"Thank you sir. Thank you."

"You're welcome."

Then I turned to walk away. She grabbed my sweater. I turned around.

"Really! Thank you sir."

"You're welcome." I turned again.

"Sir, I'm not thanking you for the money. I'm thanking you for making me think. A lot of people might help with money, but nobody ever made me solve the problem. Now I really can feed my kids. So thank you."

We both beamed at each other with big grins on our faces.

I watched her and the kids from the overpass, until the darkness took them in.

I'm Free Now

"You have entered The Wisconsin Department of Corrections Maximum Security Institution. You must remove all money, paper and coins, credit cards, jewelry, wallet or purses, anything metal, belts, shoestrings, anything hard or plastic. You may rent one of the lockboxes on the wall for $3.00 or you may leave your belongings at the desk with an officer but it is not his job to watch your things. He or she has other primary responsibilities. You may purchase up to $6.00 worth of tokens for vending machine purchases. If you are found to be in possession of any kind of controlled substance, anything that could be used as a weapon, or contraband of any kind, you will be detained for further investigation. If you have an objection to any of these conditions, it is recommended that you leave now."

Each person was asked who they were there to visit and then we waited to be called back up to the desk. It took a good while. In the mean time we visitors talked quietly among ourselves. The glaring omission in each conversation was, *"What is he in for?"* It had to be something bad, whatever it was. The time to sit in judgment was long gone. It was best not to ask. Now it was just friends and family, mostly women, mothers, grandmothers, and girlfriends, one very pregnant, who just wanted to let their loved one know that somebody still cares. Only five to seven names at a time were called. Most went to one floor. A very few went to another.

I asked a lady, *"What's on that floor?"*

"They're never coming out." she said. I kind of knew that before I asked.

We lined up, got patted down, and then went through a metal detector. It sounded off loudly when the lady in front of me went through. Two other officers showed up instantly. They pulled her to the side and checked her again. She had an under wire in her bra. She was instructed to take it off in the restroom and come back.

On through a set of bars into a space between more bars about ten feet wide and twenty feet long. The lights dimmed and a black light overhead highlighted every speck of dust and dandruff. Against the wall to the right were what seemed like three lights about 8"x 8" square. Within seconds, three faces appeared in the lights. They were windows in cell doors. For that moment, our space was dark because of the black light but their faces were perfectly framed by the light behind them. As we looked at each other, a realization swept over me. I was just as locked in as they were. Once you pass that admittance area, everybody in the whole place was locked in. It was an eerie feeling. Visitor, officer, or inmate, we were all locked in.

*****

Five years earlier my wife and I owned a retail shop in a downtown mall where we hired inner city young people 17-21 years old. Even though we had products, after a while I realized that we weren't really in the retail business. We were in the people building business. The only way to get hired was to interview with each one on the team. That could be five to eight people. If any one of them said, "*No.*" you were out. We called it '*running the gauntlet.*' My goal was to groom them to become socially conscience, service oriented business people and we were doing just that. We all wore black slacks, white shirt, and a tie every day. Vests, sweaters, and jackets were okay as long as they matched. The ladies could wear pants or a black or grey skirt if they preferred. We called each other by our last names as a gesture of respect, Mr. this or Ms. that. After a while it seemed like I was more of a mentor than their boss. They would talk to me about their lives. It wasn't just a place to work. The business gave us a reason to revolve around each other. It was a place to teach principles and virtues like responsibility, honor, and integrity. The truth is I learned far more from them than they ever learned from me.

One day a young man approached and said he wanted to work with us. His name was Will. He was a good looking guy with a welcoming smile, 5'10", 160 pounds, a braided ponytail, and a portion more muscular than most. I asked him to tell me a little bit about himself. He was 23 years old which was a little older than all of my people. He wasn't a youngster. He was a grown man, but okay. Then he said, and I quote, "*I'm a convict.*" He had done a two year bit in prison and had been out for six months.

Immediately I told him, "*No! I have young people working here. They're under my umbrella of protection. I have absolutely no intent to expose them to any kind of unwholesome activity or unsavory characters, period.*" I wished him well.

One month later he showed up again and asked if he could work with us. Again I told him no for the same reasons. I liked the guy but my team felt safe with me and I wasn't going to do anything to put their trust in jeopardy.

Two months later he came again and asked me for a job. He told me he had gone to practically every store in every mall around and had even turned down two job offers. I believed him. He certainly had enough charisma to get job offers. He said he would watch us from the balcony sometimes and loved the energy around us, the way we looked, the way we treated people, and how professional our young people carried themselves, even when they were away from the shop. He knew one of my people and they told him how much they were learning and how they felt like they were part of a team. He said that from the first time he saw us, this was the only place he wanted to work.

He said, "*Look at me. I went out and bought black pants, white shirt, and a tie. I'm dressed just like you guys. I learned how to tie a tie today before I came here. I even shaved all of the hair off of my face like you. This is the only place I want to work. I only want to work with you. Please, give me a chance.*"

Two of my team members were working that day. Another one had stopped by. All of them heard it. The silence was deafening. I pulled my team to the side and told them all I knew about the guy and how I felt about protecting them from harm. I told them about my deep reservations. Then I asked them what they thought.

Each one of them said, *"Let him run the gauntlet."* Three days later he was one of us.

He turned out to be a true leader and role model for the young ones. He was outstanding. He would come early, and work late. He paid attention not only to the mechanics of the business but also to the principles we lived by. He would want to talk with me after work. He never said it, but it was as if he wanted to study how I think. He was excited about his life. You could literally see his growth as a human being from week to week. He would come on his off days and volunteer. We'd have to send him home. It's almost like he had to pinch himself to make sure it was real. It amazed him that he could be wholesome, humble, and service oriented, and not only make money, but also be highly respected by everyone around. A new inner vision of himself was bursting to get out. The more responsibility he got, the more he thrived. And he did all of it with a smile on his face. It was like someone sprinkled pixie dust on him. He was alive. All of us saw the champion in him. He was the strongest player on the team. But underneath he struggled with his self-esteem. His eyes could see it but his heart didn't recognize the person he was becoming. As strong as he was, he was also the most fragile.

It was my practice to teach my team how to run the business. They did all of the hiring, firing, schedules, bank deposits, inventory, etc. In shopping malls, all employers actively search for good employees and they're not above stealing someone else's. I would put a pin on their collar each time one of mine got an unsolicited job offer. They had to have five before they were considered part of our team. In a two year time frame, eleven of them had twenty or more pins. Another six of them left me over time to start their own businesses. After two years I would tell them, *"You can't stay here. You have to go and grow."* Will was right on track for that kind of success.

One day a reporter approached and asked if she could write an article about our business. She wrote in the business section for the leading local newspaper. I didn't think it was a big deal to teach these young people how to run the business. They were smart. It would have been foolish not to let them run it. The collective of them was certainly smarter than the one of me. Yet apparently it was news. She interviewed several members on the team and wrote a really nice article named, "*Making Money and Making Sense.*" Will got his picture in the paper. It was a great experience for all of them. They really shined.

Three weeks later a lady called me from Australia. She had read the article and asked if I would be willing to come over there to teach what I do. Travel and expenses would be covered. My wife and I worked together in the business and she encouraged me to *'go and grow.'* She would handle things in my absence. So the first part of November, I packed my bags and went to the other side of the world.

I was gone for close to two months. It was not until I got back that my wife told me what happened. The evening before Thanksgiving she left the mall early to go to my parent's home for the holiday. They lived ninety miles away. Will and one other team member were left to close the shop. This was not unusual. Everyone on the team closed once or twice a week. Then they made the bank deposit. But this night the bank closed early. The next day was a cold and blustery Thanksgiving Day. The mall was closed and everyone went to do their holiday thing.

Will grew up there. I don't know a lot about his family but I know he had a nineteen year old sister with three kids and a younger brother in prison. The thing that none of us realized was that to him, we were his family and we had left him out there alone. No one even called him, much less invited him to dinner. As fortune would have it, he ran across a guy on the street that he had known in the joint. In a moment of weakness and feeling like no one cared, he was enticed to hit the pipe (smoke crack). Before the long weekend was over he had jacked two cars with a toy gun, blown the deposit money on drugs, gotten caught, locked up, and was waiting to go before the judge.

Needless to say, all of us were saddened, disappointed, angry, and a host of other sentiments about Will. It was a body blow to our team. We marched on but with a little less joy for some time. In the meantime, he was sitting it out in the jail house for two or three months until trial. Life was getting back to normal and that would have been the end of it except for one thing. On the day before his trial, his girlfriend came to the mall to see me. She told me that for him to do another bit in the joint didn't bother him nearly as much as violating the trust with me. She was a sweet girl. Her parents never liked him being in her life. She couldn't ask her parents to go. So she came to ask me if I would go to court with her to see his trial. I agreed.

At court there is a set time for each trial but for all intents and purposes it's just a very rough estimate. They call the case and then the bailiff brings out one Black or Latino man after another with your odd White guy sprinkled in from time to time. All in custody wear an orange jump suit and shackles. There is a chain around the waist with hands cuffed in front. The chain goes down to two ankle extensions and the prisoners shuffle in like penguins. For the judge it seemed 'work a day routine,' like a teacher grading papers. He would barely look up sometimes before dispensing years of 'however I feel today' justice on the shackled person's life.

Finally Will's case got called. The judges' chair was up high so it made everybody else look small. When Will shuffled out he looked over and smiled at us. No one from his family was there. The judge read the charges, *"Two counts of carjacking with consideration that the gun was a toy."* He asked for a plea.

"Guilty your honor. I plead for mercy from the court."

"Does anyone have something to say either for or against this man before I rule?"

He looked over his glasses for a response. Will looked over at me. The judge raised his gavel and I raised my hand at the same time. He pointed the gavel at me. *"Stand up. State your name and your relationship to the defendant. What say you?"*

"My name is JRS and I was his employer."

"Has the defendant wronged you in any way?"

"Yes sir. He stole five hundred dollars from me but that's not what I want to talk about. The man in the orange jumpsuit and shackles is not the man I know. I know the man who came to work every day on time, did his job, and then went the extra mile on a regular basis. He wore black slacks, white shirt, and a tie every day, as we all did. He was a leader with a word of encouragement in his mouth for all who came near. He was a true professional and a credit to the retail community. I was proud to have him in my employ. I don't know what happened to the man I know. But I humbly request that you pronounce sentence on the man I know, and not this man in the jumpsuit and shackles."

The judge looked at Will with his gavel raised high and said, *"Because of your previous criminal record and the fact that even though the gun was a toy, it was still two counts of armed robbery, I was going to sentence you to two twenty year terms to run consecutively (one after the other). But because of this man who spoke so well of the man he knows, I sentence you to two twenty year terms to run concurrently (at the same time). Look over and thank that man."* Bam! He struck the gavel.

As Will was led off, he turned and looked at us with tears in his eyes and silently mouthed, *"Thank you."*

*****

A year and a half later my father died. My wife and I closed the business and moved back home to take care of my aging mother. We didn't want her to have to move off of the land she had been on since she was seven years old. She was seventy-seven then. I had a different life. I worked part time and had a business that I ran from home. My wife worked part time as well, and we both took care of mom. It was a big step down financially but it was a labor of love and done without regret.

From time to time over the next four years we would get long letters from Will. There would always be a money order included with anywhere from four to seven dollars. He was making an effort to pay me back. I was blown away by the integrity it took to do that. He would also mention that he had put my name on his visitors list. My wife and I would read these letters and smile but we never replied. It was like we had these children that claimed us. Will happened to be our bad boy. But he claimed us too. One summer I went through a three week stretch when I couldn't get Will out of my mind. On a Friday night I told my wife that in the morning I was going up north to visit Will.

I looked it up on the map. The prison town was far away in the middle of nowhere. At least three to four hours away. I got up before sunrise and hit the road. I got there around 9:00 a.m. and stopped for breakfast before heading over to the place. There are three or four prisons in that little bitty rural town. There's a whole prison industrial complex there. Prisons are the economic engine and growth industry that drive the place. I would bet they have a far greater Black and Latino population than White but you'd never see them because they're all locked up. The town had a foreboding, slave ship, plantation kind of feel for me. Even though it was a beautiful Saturday morning, it felt like going into the deep woods where shadow and shade rule the day, where no sunshine hits the ground. I wondered how many other towns there are like this across America.

*****

"You have entered The Wisconsin Department of Corrections Maximum Security Institution..."

Finally I got to the big visitors room where I waited about ten minutes for Will. The room was divided into two sections. Three fourths of the room was open with tables, chairs, and a couple of couches. There were several vending machines on the back wall. If you sit at a table, you must have your hands on the table. Wherever you sit you must have your hands in plain sight at all times. You can touch briefly, like shaking hands or a quick embrace. Anything more and you will be escorted out promptly. The other one fourth of the room was against the wall with a glass partition and telephones. You must sit, not stand, at a station and pick up the phone to talk to your party. People would put their hands on the glass to simulate a touch. Yes, they really do that. There were thirty people total with six guards in the room. An inmate could have no more than one guest at a time. Your visit is twenty minutes. Then you must to go.

Will had no idea who had come to visit so he was shocked to see me. We hugged each other slightly longer than briefly until a guard tapped me on the shoulder and reminded me of the rules. We just smiled and laughed for another minute or two. He was leaner now and his hair was short. He asked about my wife with affection, and who on our team we were still in touch with. I bought a few candy bars with my tokens. He hadn't eaten one in months. I've never seen anyone enjoy a candy bar that much. He worked in the laundry where he made .08 cents an hour. It took him two years to get that job. He was happy to be working because it gave him something to do and he gets paid for it. Otherwise he would just sit in his cell, forever. There was a man with a Polaroid camera (a trustee-an inmate being rewarded for good behavior but who may or may not be respected by other inmates). We took three pictures together at a dollar each: One shaking hands, one with hard looks on our faces, and one with smiles he wanted my wife to have. It was a playful moment with two old friends horsing around. Will insisted on paying. That was a week's pay for him. He took pride in it, as a gracious host would. Half of our time was gone so we took a seat. Then Will began to speak.

With all seriousness he said, "*You don't know how much I've hated you. You ruined my life. Before you, I knew who I was, a convict. I told you that. I was clear about what was expected of me so I could do whatever I wanted. Nobody cared much about me,*

165

and I didn't care much about myself. I thought kindness and humility were for the weak. Only punks served other people by choice. I ain't no punk. And then I met you. I never cared about a job before. You taught us values and principles to live by. We couldn't just leave that stuff at work. You treated us like we were important, like family. You paid to get one of our team member's car fixed so he could get to school and come to work. You bought one a prom dress and got her hair done. You bought groceries for another one who had kids. You didn't say anything about it but they did. All you saw was the good in us. You expected more of us than we did of ourselves and forced us to be better people. You gave me responsibility. You trusted me. Nobody ever trusted me. What am I supposed to do with that? What am I supposed to think about that? How am I supposed to carry that around in here?

I got a library card. It has become my most prized possession. I've read over 150 books. I can tell you about the ancient civilizations, the Greeks, Rome, the Renaissance, Slavery, the American Revolution, and the Civil War, from Ulysses to Malcolm X, and how the government works with the balance of power."

He sat up strait. "*I couldn't go back to who I was. I'm not a convict anymore. I'm an educated man. I'm at peace with the world. Thank you Mr. Summers for helping me find myself.*"

Then the buzzer rang. It was time to go.

We stood up and embraced. Visitors were heading for the door. With head up, standing erect, and a look of assurance on his face he said, "*I'm free now. I just have to get out of here!*"

THE END